Spiritual Insights of T. W. Willingham

Book 10

Crumbs About Prayer and Obedience

Crumbs About Prayer and Obedience

Beacon Hill Press of Kansas City
Kansas City, Missouri

Contents

Foreword

Dr. T. W. Willingham is almost a legend in the Church of the Nazarene. He has served as pastor, district superintendent, college president, and executive at the world headquarters of the church.

Somewhat like Bernard Baruch he has been a close advisor to general superintendents and fledgling executive directors over the years. His business acumen and practical judgment have been sought after by all of us.

His greatest impact, however, has been in the spiritual realm. I and literally thousands have been stimulated by his insight into the Scriptures. Take these "crumbs," which I consider the most prophetic (prophetlike) pieces that have ever come from our presses, and revel in them.

—M. A. (Bud) Lunn

A Note of Thanks

First, I desire to thank my God for giving me time, strength, and guidance during the past 40 years as I have worked on the 16 books that I have had published.

In 1970, the Lord gave me a five-page directive concerning my writings in which He said, "I have given you two helpers . . . and it is My desire that they help you, and if they abide near Me they will feel the same way."

These two God-given workers—Clara Rogers and Kathy Butts—have been dependable and efficient and, more important, have felt that in so laboring they have been serving the Master and His kingdom.

Clara has corrected nearly all my handwritten articles, as well as typing many. Kathy has typed much, organized material, and by research and study, has made many valuable contributions. I thank God for both of them; without such help my work could not have been done.

If these messages prove to be of spiritual help to you, just give all the praise to our Heavenly Father.

—T. W. WILLINGHAM

I Just Came By to Talk with You

Many mornings have I been called into wakefulness with the familiar words, "I just came by to talk with you." I might brush this greeting from my mind but for the fact that not once that I can remember did the Speaker break faith with His expressed purpose.

In these early morning periods, I have received instruction for the day—and at times, correction, rebuke, and encouragement. From the Visitor I have received such help, information, and guidance as only a heavenly Ambassador could impart. These early morning vigils have become highlights of my days, the guideposts for my journey, the storehouse of my strength.

Is it a strange thing that a heavenly Guest should visit a son in the 20th century, when He began to converse with His own "in the cool of the day" millennia ago (Gen. 3:8)?

The repetition of such visits hinges upon one's desire for them and the faithfulness in which the advice, counsel, and direction given is heeded.

The statement "The meek will he guide in judgment" (Ps. 25:9) argues His purpose to guide those who thus qualify. The Holy Spirit has been promised as a Teacher, but no teacher can instruct a preoccupied pupil. There must be a desire to learn and a purpose to apply what is learned. One fails to grasp the full meaning of such visitations if he attributes their pleasure and benefits solely to the Visitor. Although the benefits to Him cannot be overestimated, nevertheless there is value and, I believe, pleasure to the visited as well.

The purposes of such encounters are not all intended for the benefit of the one visited, however. The Visitor has work to be done, important tasks to be performed; and He is in need of assistants, men who are informed as to the tasks to be carried out, the schedule of their performance, and the ends that are to be attained by their execution.

"I must work the works of him that sent me" (John 9:4). These words were spoken by the Son when He was one of us and among us. Could He have performed such tasks in a manner acceptable to the Father without instruction from Him? Much less can we without His guidance! He operates a school of instruction, and the Teacher is never late to His classes. If this program of spiritual education lags or is discontinued, charge not the failure to the Instructor but to the truant pupil.

The early morning visits of the Teacher have been fairly well established as a pattern of His dealing with me. No other moments of the day are so precious, and no other instruction so meaningful.

I record this message for two reasons. First, I desire to give testimony to an experience that has become so meaningful to me; and second, I desire to encourage my readers to seek to establish such relationship with the Teacher.

Be assured that I do not think myself to be a favorite son to whom alone the great Teacher deigns to come. The Heavenly Father's heart yearns for such fellowship with His own. The infinite Spirit has time for every finite soul; He can diffuse His infinite presence throughout all space and speak to all His creatures simultaneously, imparting divergent messages at the same moment. A million different petitioners imploring divine guidance on as many subjects cannot confuse our Creator, and to answer each in clarity simultaneously would not tax His ingenuity. There is room for all of us in His early morning school.

Until our dealings with God become personalized, they are vague, uncertain, and lacking in spiritual power. Not until one hears His voice for himself does the true meaning of the "living God" become understandable. It is this living, personal message from a knowable God that makes the heart radiate with light, the spiritual muscles flex in confidence, and the day's toil become meaningful.

If one asks, "How may I know that the words thus spoken are the words of Another, and not the echo of my own subconscious self?" the answer is clear. In the ensuing conversations, revelations of truth are often made—at times, unthought-of events not yet enacted are brought into mind. Promises are often received involving future happenings that only a Higher Authority could know.

The accuracy of such revelations, especially of future events, can be tested by history when fulfillment has verified them. When one has had occasion to check hundreds of such items over a span of years, and has found that 100 percent of them have been true, he becomes a firm believer in the speaking Spirit.

It takes time to cultivate a friendship with men, and it is no different with God; the time need not be long. It can become fruitful and enjoyable at the very beginning of the Christian career, but it grows in intimacy with application accompanied by obedience. To willfully ignore the leadings of the Spirit is to discourage His return. There must be a willingness to obey if one is to get His directions.

The speaking Spirit is ever speaking, but the dull of hearing do not always comprehend the message. To the listening soul He always comes, and to the obedient He speaks again and again.

11

I am ever inviting Him to come again; His tender Spirit responds to our love. He can be grieved by our neglect but will respond to our loving call.

Thank You, Heavenly Visitor. Come often and stay longer is my prayer. Thy voice I will obey.

The Acme of Prayer

There are many types of prayer referred to in the Word, all of which are to be commended and practiced: prayers in the congregation, in small groups, and where only two are thus engaged; but none of these represent the highest type of prayer.

Jesus announced the highest form when He said, "But thou, when thou prayest, enter into thy closet, and when thou hast shut thy door, pray to thy Father which is in secret; and thy Father which seeth in secret shall reward thee openly" (Matt. 6:6).

In the masterpiece of His teaching, the Sermon on the Mount, Jesus placed this most direct message on the manner of prayer.

"Thy closet" marks the place of solitude and aloneness; the "shut . . . door" excludes all others; and "secret" further emphasizes seclusion. Here the Father, and the Father alone, sees. One is perfectly free to open to the depths, for no other eye can see, and no other ear can hear.

The deepest and most vital things of the soul cannot be safely shared with anyone but God. He alone will remain always faithful and true; others could fail.

The very commandment indicates that there are deep secrets of the soul that should be shared, and we are invited to share them with God. There is nothing about us that He does not know. Then why tell Him? The things that He knows in His own right are known without our consent. I have no credit for His knowledge of them. He knows even if

I object to His knowing. When I share them with Him, I am expressing my willingness for Him to know. He now knows them with my consent. I have given them to Him. I relinquish my hold on them.

One cannot safely tell the Lord all that disturbs his soul in the presence of others; hence, the need of the "closet." In this closed closet, one may completely open his soul to God without fear. He can tell Him all: good and bad, his faith and his doubts, his love and his sin.

Here one gets a release by releasing. He comes away relaxed, for he has told the whole to One who cares. Here he can face the verdict of the Judge with no onlookers and walk out, knowing that the case is closed forever.

In the closet the pressures of life are laid aside, and the advices of men are put on trial. In the presence of the all-knowing One, our own judgments and the judgments of others may be checked and true guidance found.

The promise for such praying is that He "shall reward thee openly." The nature of the reward is not stated, but it will come, and any divine reward is worthwhile.

Jesus not only gave this advice to His followers but also practiced this pattern of prayer himself. Aloneness with the Father took much of His time, and the outward awards are known to all who read His story.

To be alone with another is a mark of love, and love is the highest commandment. In giving these instructions on prayer, Jesus was saying in other terms, "Thou shalt love the Lord thy God," for love leads to aloneness with the object of our love.

If what we have just said be true, what must be said of the one who desires no secret meeting with his Master, no closet retreat in his home?

To have a secret shared with you is a great privilege; the greater the secret, the greater the honor. God has secrets to share with each of His children, and "the secret of the Lord is with them that fear him" (Ps. 25:14). If it is a secret for us, it must be shared with us when we are alone; hence, the closed door.

It is in the closet that one gets new insights into God and the things of God. God is infinite and His ways past finding out, but in the secret place He reveals to us what we can in no way learn otherwise. Why should He show His secrets to those who have no appreciation of them? Our desire to be alone with Him is a revelation of our love for Him and our desire to know what He has to say to us.

This closet meeting is a means of renewing our strength. Life makes so many drafts on our energies that we soon become exhausted. In the closet we meet the Renewer of our strength and are prepared for the duties of another day.

This closet meeting is a confession of our utter dependence upon Another. If we feel no need of His help, we will probably bypass the closet; but if our need is ever before us, we will make repeated use of it.

This closet meeting is also a declaration of our faith in Him. Why would one thus retreat except that he believed that the reward promised would be forthcoming? The very going is the faith necessary to the receiving.

Since this closet relationship is so important, should we be surprised that Satan devises so many means to rob us of its benefits? The "cares of this world, and the deceitfulness of riches" (Matt. 13:22; Mark 4:19) crowd heavily and constantly upon us and often snatch from us this pearl of great price.

The practice of the secret place will qualify us for the other types of praying so much needed. It will also equip us for a more useful service among men. It is not a retreat from others but a preparation for a meaningful ministry among them.

Note how it worked in the life of the Master. No one was more alone with the Father than was Jesus, and yet no one was involved with humanity more than He. Instead of being mutually exclusive, they are complementary; the one prepared for the other.

The open reward promised is exemplified in the Savior's life. Who had more outward rewards from the Father than did He? He spoke with authority; He worked the works of God and successfully challenged the enemies of righteousness. In life He was dauntless; in temptation He was victorious; in rejection He was forgiving; in death He was loving; and in eternity He is Lord of all. He faithfully used the closed closet and reaped the plenteous reward, rewards that men and angels witnessed and shall through endless ages.

Jesus was opening the gates to the very acme of prayer—the intimate aloneness with His Father. It stands ajar to all who care to enter, and those who do are blessed. But thou, when thou prayest, enter, close, pray, and be rewarded.

What I Say to God Is Secondary

What I say to God is important, but it is not all-important. God's word is final, therefore all-important.

Perhaps it is the failure to realize this fact that renders our prayers less meaningful than they could be. Often our prayer period is consumed almost completely by what we have to say. We may divide our message into thanksgiving and adoration as well as petition, but when the total is taken, we have filled the time with our own message.

It is not unlike the case of a pupil entering the classroom to spend the entire period carrying on conversation and then leaving, having heard nothing from the teacher.

When our prayer time is over, what have we heard from God? One may answer, "I felt blessed; I laid all my cares at His feet; I pledged continued allegiance; I trust Him to work everything out." All of this is good, but what did He say? Did He say anything? Did you expect Him to speak? Did you give Him time to speak?

When one consumes the hour himself, he must feel that what he has to say is the most important thing; and having done that which is of greatest value, he may then arise and go. When one thus conducts his prayer life, what basis has he for faith for the tasks to be done? What guidance has he received? When he arises to go, whose duties is he going out to perform? Is he just seeking power to execute his already-formulated plans, or is he seeking an unfolding of the Master's plan? In short, what guidance has he received?

It must be remembered that all faith is based upon the message received from God and not on the one conveyed by us. It matters but little what we have said, if there is no response from Him. What He says is the basis—the only basis —of faith. The act of power is the one ordered by the Lord, the task can be performed if it has been ordered by Him.

This listening time is perhaps the most neglected. One must expect a response if he is to get it, and time must be given for God to speak. "Speak, Lord; for thy servant heareth" is a great prayer that should be universally employed (1 Sam. 3:9-10).

This listening is seen in the life of Christ and the Holy Spirit. Jesus said, "As I hear, I judge"; "I speak that which I have seen with my Father" (John 5:30; 8:38). Time was given for the Father's message, for the extensive prayer life of Jesus was not a one-sided matter. He didn't do all the talking; He also listened.

The Holy Spirit followed the same pattern. Of Him, Jesus said, "Whatsoever he shall hear, that shall he speak" (John 16:13). The very fact that both the Son and the Spirit listened should be proof enough for us to see our need for listening.

Someone may say, "I just take the written Word and stand on that. I believe all that is written and choose my promise and go ahead." It is interesting to note that Jesus did not conduct His life on this basis. He knew all of His Father's written promises better than we know them, and yet He listened, that He might "rightly divid[e] the word of truth" (2 Tim. 2:15). The written Word must be moved upon by the Spirit and made to speak a living message to us. "The letter killeth, but the spirit giveth life" (2 Cor. 3:6).

Unless we listen, we may seize upon the wrong promise for our need at that time. The Spirit is needed to speak

18

through the Word and make it live for us. Then we have the living Word of His selection and not one of our own.

In true prayer we allow the Teacher to teach the lesson of His own choosing. We pray to be told and not to tell. Telling is secondary; the final answer rests with God, and one must wait for it.

If only one could get His message, hear Him say, "This is the way; this is what I want you to do," he would be invincible. The disciples' failure to hear Jesus' purpose, "Let us go over unto the other side" (Luke 8:22; cf. Mark 4:35), caused them to be faithless and frightened. His will had been stated —"the other side" for "us"; no storm could cancel out that announced destination. They had a basis for faith—His word. There they should have stood in faith and let the weary Master sleep. They had been occupied with their own thoughts and took no time to listen or at least to digest His message to them.

All faith arises from what He says. Faith to do the impossible can only come from what He says to us for the time at hand. Nothing is impossible to a faith that is based upon what He says. Another time when He told Peter, "Come," Peter had faith to walk the waves (Matt. 14:29). Faith may embrace anything and accomplish it, if He has said so. What He says is, therefore, the important thing.

Without reasonable doubt, our prayer periods should be rescheduled. Do we desire to do exploits for Him? Do we wish to achieve in His name? We can accomplish any task, however difficult; overcome any obstacle, however great; if we can only have faith for it. Jesus made that perfectly clear: "If ye have faith as a grain of mustard seed, ye shall say . . . and it shall [be done]" (Matt. 17:20).

Just have faith and speak. It seems so easy, yet who is doing it? Who is doing much more than a man-size job? Where does the God of the impossible appear? We look almost in vain to see Him in our achievements; by and large our tasks are man-size, not God-size. Faith can span that gap. But how? Where can I get such faith? There is but one way: "Faith cometh by hearing," not by speaking ourselves, but from the speaking God (Rom. 10:17). The listening is the secret.

When we move from the role of the speaker to the role of the listener, we open the door for the Teacher; and having been taught, we can go out to teach. When tasks have been ordered, faith can perform them—with ease and joy.

Whose Ear Is Heavy?

When the conversation lags and fades into emptiness, someone has grown "dull of hearing." Since only God and ourselves are involved in this conversing, if the conversation has come to a standstill, one or the other is at fault.

Let God speak for himself: "Behold, the Lord's hand is not shortened, that it cannot save; neither his ear heavy, that it cannot hear" (Isa. 59:1). The Psalmist vindicates his Maker: "Behold, he that keepeth Israel shall neither slumber nor sleep" (Ps. 121:4). Isaiah goes even further and declares, "The Creator . . . fainteth not, neither is weary" (Isa. 40:28).

It is evident that if the conversation has faded away, the failure cannot be charged to the Almighty. We must look to the only other participant—ourselves—for the cause, and if we are interested in renewing the conversation, that we must do.

Repeatedly have we been warned of the danger of growing "dull of hearing," and the causes for it. Jesus found His generation "dull of hearing" (Matt. 13:15), and He asked, "Having ears, hear ye not?" (Mark 8:18). Even the disciples grew listless. The writer of the Hebrews letter found himself handicapped, "seeing ye are dull of hearing" (5:11).

Poor spiritual hearing has been an agelong handicap that the prophets and Christ have had to cope with. We are living in an opiate-laden atmosphere; the spiritual air is filled with the smog of doubt, and we are constantly breathing the air of rebellion. We are in need of a constant awakening lest we sleep the sleep of death. Even in Gethsemane, the disciples went to sleep, and this in the face of Christ's earnest words: "My soul is exceeding sorrowful, even unto death: tarry ye here, and watch with me" (Matt. 26:38).

The picture of the last days drawn by Jesus is that of the 10 virgins: "They all slumbered and slept"—the wise and the foolish; five asleep and lost, five asleep but safe, but all asleep (Matt. 25:1-5). Thus will time's closing night enshroud all mankind. Jesus said that for the "elect's sake" those days would be shortened (24:22).

In a darkening age, we need to "exhort one another daily" (Heb. 3:13), that we do not "sleep, as do others" (1 Thess. 5:6). The apostle Peter, who himself slept in Gethsemane, found it necessary to write to others, "Yea, I think it meet, as long as I am in this tabernacle, to stir you up by putting you in remembrance" (2 Pet. 1:13). In both of his Epistles, he stirred up their minds on these things and promised to leave his warning on record after his decease.

If the fault of poor communication is not with God, we should take the responsibility of clearing our own skirts. We have been warned of what bedims our eyes and dulls our ears, and are warned against allowing it.

Jesus set forth some of the causes of such failures in His parables; in His parable of the sower (Matt. 13:18), "the care of this world" is mentioned as one of the chief offenders. Just the multiplicity of the ordinary duties of life take up the time and drown out the voices from above. The humdrum of life deadens the ear, the sensitivity to spiritual things wears away, and only a rumbling sound is heard. The voice from above now becomes as thunder, and the message has lost its meaning.

The prophet lays a much graver charge against Israel and attributes their problem to their sins. In fact, he tells us that because of their sins, God will not hear them (Isa. 59:2).

If sin is not the cause, then it is possible that the very rush, noise, and multiplicity of duties—even duties in King-

22

dom work—benumb one's hearing. We become so accustomed to the tumult that we can't hear the still, small voice of the Shepherd.

This seems to have been the problem of Elijah; he was a man of thunders, floods, fires, and blood, and when God tried to show him another way, he could scarcely comprehend. God sent a mountain-rending wind, but He was not in it. Then came an earthquake, but God wasn't in it. Then a fire, but God wasn't in it either. Then the still voice of God. The old prophet appeared to be unable to make the transition, so God sent him on to anoint Elisha in his room, and took the old prophet to heaven. Elisha did twice the miracles that the fire-calling Elijah did. The thunder of activity can dull our sense of the speaking Spirit and keep us from the higher accomplishments for God.

The Messiah points the way to clarity of hearing. Of Him it was said that "opening the ears, . . . he heareth not" (Isa. 42:20). He learned to hear by the process of elimination; He crowded out the noises and demands of earth that He might hear the whispers of His Father. He kept His ear attuned to the Voice from the skies and quickly heeded its message.

Perhaps the most prolific source of dull hearing is heedlessness. "If ye will hear his voice, harden not your hearts" (Heb. 3:15) is the divine advice. The process of hardening begins when light comes and one hesitates to walk in it. He then begins to harden himself against God, and "Who hath hardened himself against him, and hath prospered?" (Job 9:4).

Ignoring the calls of God immunizes one's soul against Him. The heavenly Voice, unheeded, grows dimmer and sounds in the end like a fading echo. By not heeding, one comes to the place where "hearing ye shall hear, and shall not understand" (Matt. 13:14).

If there is coming to us no message from the skies, no call to the higher, no urge upward, we should give heed as to how we are listening and to whom. The call of the adversary would drown out the call of the Shepherd, and if oft listened to, it becomes the familiar voice and is taken for our guide.

The deceitfulness of sin is an ever-pressing problem, and the calls to its luring paths ring ever in our ears. It is only by diligent search and close application that we can maintain a tuning to the Voice from above. Our hearing must be kept keen and attuned to the "still small voice" (1 Kings 19:12). The clamor of the common must be exchanged for the quiet of the lofty.

God Seldom Hears
My Prayers

The subject of this meditation is not a statement to arouse debate, incur criticism, create distrust in myself, or appear sensational. It is a sober statement of fact.

The biblical background for this meditation is found in the words of John: "And this is the confidence that we have in him, that, if we ask any thing according to his will, he heareth us: And if we know that he hear us, whatsoever we ask, we know that we have the petitions that we desired of him" (1 John 5:14-15).

If one hears much praying in which petitions are made, and is a close observer of the results that follow, he will find himself in no disagreement with the thesis, "God Seldom Hears My Prayers."

Perhaps our problem is that we do not think. This was the charge God made against His people a long time ago through the ministry of Isaiah:

"The ox knoweth his owner, and the ass his master's crib: but Israel doth not know, my people do not take time to think" (Isa. 1:3, margin).

If people would take time to think, they would know that God hears but few prayers.

A number of times I have shocked congregations with the statement that God seldom hears my prayer, when only five minutes before my statement some minister had prayed a very earnest prayer in which he made several requests, none of which were heard. He may have prayed for God to send a much-needed rain that day, or that there would be seekers at the close of the service. Neither happened. Did God hear those prayers? According to John, He did not. Note John's words:

"If we know that he hear us, whatsoever we ask, we know that we have the petitions that we desired of him."

Let us not be afraid to look this passage squarely in the face. In honestly looking, it may at first appear that the value of prayer will be completely demolished. That is not true. Only error is made to perish. We cannot injure our faith by being honest with God and His Word. Presumption and false ideas will suffer, but we must uproot the false before we can establish the true. This was Jeremiah's commission and a commission of all of God's followers.

Did God hear the prayer referred to above? The Word says that if God hears, we get the petitions that we desired of Him—not some substitute blessing, but "whatsoever we ask."

Since the pray-er did not get the petitions that he desired of God, then God did not hear the prayer. It seems that nothing could be more plainly stated, and facts bear out that conclusion.

It should be noted before we go further that Christ uses the words "see" and "hear" in two different senses. This is illustrated by Jesus in Matthew's Gospel. Jesus, referring to some of His listeners, said, "They seeing see not; and hearing they hear not" (Matt. 13:13). In the first instance, Jesus said that they saw and they heard. Then He said that they did not see or hear. His meaning is clear; they were hearing the words that He spoke, but not heeding them.

We all know that in the first meaning of the words "seeing" and "hearing," God sees and hears everything. He hears our cursing. He hears our denial of His deity. No word is

26

uttered that He does not hear in the context of the Word "hearing" as it is first used.

The meaning of "hearing" as Jesus used it in the second case involves paying attention to, listening to, and acting upon. The petitions made in the prayer under consideration were not heeded by the Lord, were not granted—in short, were not "heard."

The important point in this whole matter is the statement "If we know that he hear us." If we know that, then we know we have our request no matter what it is. That is the plain statement of the text.

Again we ask, When do we know that He has heard? I know no way that I can know that God has heard me when I make a request of Him except that He himself tells me that He has heard. I cannot go on a good feeling. The blessing of the Lord may be greatly felt by the one who is praying and by all who are in the audience, but that is no assurance that the petitions made will be granted. We must know that He has heard us in the sense above described.

May I add my personal testimony. In all the years of my Christian life (now 72), I have never, when making petitions, had the Spirit of God say to me, "I have heard you," that I failed to receive the very thing asked for.

I repeat, God seldom hears my prayers. The petitions that I have made were numerous and varied. I have prayed for thousands of things that I have never received. This is also true of others whose prayers I have listened to for nearly three-quarters of a century.

Here we are brought face-to-face with the necessity of understanding the living God. There can be no such assuring response as we are discussing except from a living, speaking God.

This passage of Scripture under consideration should open up to us the necessity of cultivating an intimate relationship with the Spirit, that we may the more often have the assurance from Him that He has heard and heeded our requests. If He tells us that He has heard, the answer is on the way, and its arrival is certain.

From the many passages in the Word of God on prayer, it is well established that it would please God for His children to maintain such a relationship with Him that answered prayer would not be the unusual. Whatever progress is made must be made through a closer relationship with the living, speaking God. It takes time to get acquainted with Him, and most of us are too much engaged in other things to come to know Him as One who can speak to us and assure us of what He is going to do.

If we would be more honest about this business of unanswered prayers, it would lay the foundation for a sincere approach to a real prayer life in which—more and more—answers would be assured. May God in His mercy help us all at this point.

Meaningless Mottoes

The Lord reminded the prophet Ezekiel that His word to the people was as "a very lovely song of one that hath a pleasant voice . . . they hear thy words, but they do them not" (Ezek. 33:32). The message was divinely inspired and sent, but to them it was meaningless.

To be perfectly frank—more frank than we care to be unless divinely aided—there are great promises of God that hang on the walls of our memories like gilded mottoes that we would not remove for any amount of money, and yet for all practical purposes they are meaningless to us; glowing promises but void of fulfillment.

There are many such, but let us note three of them: (1) "If ye shall ask any thing in my name, I will do it" (John 14:14); (2) "Whatsoever ye shall ask in my name, that will I do" (v. 13); (3) "If ye abide in me, and my words abide in you, ye shall ask what ye will, and it shall be done unto you" (15:7).

Take the last-mentioned promise: "Ye shall ask what ye will, and it shall be done unto you." The promise is limitless. True, it is conditional; yet it is limitless: "ask what ye will."

Here what one gets is determined by his own asking. There is no limit. The first verse says, "Ask any thing," and the second says, "Whatsoever ye shall ask." I see no way that a promise could be more all-inclusive and more fully substantiated than are these. We quote them often and hang them high on the walls; they are pleasant to our ears, like the

29

message of the ancient prophet, but are they not as meaningless?

Honestly—if you are willing to be so—do you know what it is to "ask what you will" and get it? Does your own will determine what you get from God? I must confess I know but little about this kind of asking. In fact, I would hesitate to say just how little I do know about it.

In the light of such admission on my part, I ask myself, Are these promises to be accepted as they are written? Can one reach the place where he can "ask what [he] will" and get it? Or are these the pictures of ideal heights that can never be reached and are hung before us to reveal our imperfections and place us guilty before God? Are these promises to serve as the ancient law that could only condemn and never save?

Are we here being reminded that the answerable asking is forever beyond our reach, and therefore we must trust His asking and ignore our own? Just what do these promises mean? Do they mean anything? Since they are beyond us, shall we forget them? Should it be well to forget them? And shall we forget all the others that appear no more real than these?

In my perfectly honest moments these questions are not empty and meaningless words, but they are soul-searching and challenging questions.

It is true, and already observed, that these promises are based upon certain conditions; but then again we have the opportunity of brushing them aside as being meaningless because they are based on conditions that are beyond our reach. These conditions are, "If ye abide in me, and my words abide in you," and "if ye shall ask . . . in my name." Are these conditions reachable? If not, we have meaningful promises rendered meaningless because conditioned upon impossible attainments.

Should we allow these great promises to continue to hang as "meaningless mottoes" on the walls of our soul, or should they become movers of miracles in our present lives? Frankly, I cannot brush them aside without, in the same stroke, discarding all that the Master has said in other places.

Honesty of mind, as well as the pull of my heart, tells me that here lies the unused power of prayer, beckoning all of us to seek her as silver and exercise it "that the Father may be glorified in the Son" (John 14:13). This last statement is a golden key to these resources of prayer. Too often we think of prayer's power and what it can achieve instead of the honor that this kind of asking brings to the Father through the Son.

The Son is waiting for the kind of asking that will allow Him to glorify His Father, and that kind of asking is the asking in His name. Here we stand at the portal of power. When we ask in His name we enter.

What then is meant by asking in His name, that asking which gets "any thing" it asks for? If we can answer this question and apply the answer, we are well on our way to divine success.

The first step in asking in the name of another is to completely identify oneself with the other. Thus all self-originating ideas and desires must be identical with those of the other, brought in line with His or else abandoned.

To ask in the name of Another is to be moved in the asking by the mind and the spirit of the other. The asking has then become His asking—ours by adoption. When His spirit completely dominates our spirit, His thoughts become our thoughts, and His asking becomes our asking. Jesus said, "He that hath seen me hath seen the Father" (John 14:9). In like manner, when we are totally yielded to His Son so that His Son can perfectly express himself through us, then when the Father hears us praying, He hears the prayer of the Son, and the Son's prayer is answerable.

Desire, insofar as it is personal, must be transmuted into His desire, for no desire contrary to His has value, and no request outside of His will can have His answer.

31

The death-life process takes over here—we die to our desires that we may live in His. Here faith is born. It is not difficult for one to believe that the Father will answer the Son's prayers, and when we know that our asking is the Son's asking, faith is spontaneous. The key to these promises is Christlikeness in nature and mind. Then the meaningless mottoes become means of miracles.

The Limitations of Prayer

"If ye shall ask any thing in my name, I will do it"
(John 14:14).

This seems to be a simple and all-inclusive promise. That it is true, there can be no question. It was spoken by Jesus himself, and He dealt exclusively in truth.

If, in my earlier ministry, I had drawn a theme from this text, it likely would have been "The Limitless Possibilities of Prayer." But in my later ministry, after more thought, I have used the same text with the theme "The *Limitations* of Prayer." Quite a contrast in the themes, and yet both come from the same text!

It is evident that the meaning here is more than to conclude one's prayer with the words, "This we ask in Jesus' name." We know that this is not the meaning, for those of us who have been praying and listening to the prayers of hundreds of other people know that most of the requests made in the prayers ending with this phrase were not answered.

However, there is no reason for one to alter such a closing statement. It is a good form and at times has meaning, but in most cases it is but a form. The ungranted requests are proofs of that.

What is really meant by asking in the name of Jesus? Since it is more than to append the phrase "This we ask in Jesus' name," what does it mean? In other words, when do we thus ask?

The undeniable promise of Jesus is that such asking will

be rewarded by a definite response: "I will do it"—not something else, but "it"—the very thing requested.

The disciples to whom Jesus gave this promise did not understand that asking in His name was to append that expression to their prayers; this is evident from the fact that of the more than 70 prayers recorded, or referred to, in the New Testament after the resurrection of Christ, not one of them is concluded with the phrase "In the name of Jesus Christ," so commonly used by us today. Two of these prayers close with a kindred expression, but none of the others use it or any modified form thereof. This form is but another of the traditions of the elders that has been passed down to us.

In thus speaking, we are in no way discouraging the ending of our prayers in this way. It is a good form, but not a Christ-taught form nor a form practiced by the apostles and other Christians who have left for us a record of their praying in the Word of God.

The purpose of debunking this false idea is to disabuse our minds of the thought that having enthusiastically lifted our prayer to God and closed with the phrase "This we ask in the name of Jesus," we have met the condition on which is made His promise, "I will do it." The meaning lies deeper than that. That we know, for this kind of asking does not work. Some prayers to which this closing is attached may be answered, but the answer will not come just because of such attachment.

Some seem to feel that this phrase is a sort of talisman of power and when waved before God, will assure the fulfillment of their requests. This error is shown very clearly by an incident recorded in Acts 19. When "God wrought special miracles by the hands of Paul" (v. 11), some others thought that they could use the name of Jesus as a sort of magic wand to accomplish the same thing.

"Then certain of the vagabond Jews, exorcists, took upon them to call over them which had evil spirits the name of the Lord Jesus . . . And the evil spirit answered and said, Jesus I know, and Paul I know; but who are ye?" (vv. 13, 15).

Then followed the beating, and the running (v. 16). They soon found out that the use of the name of Jesus was no magic wand that anyone could use to get his desires and requests fulfilled.

Before going further, we would like to add support to the proof text to substantiate the fact beyond any doubt that Jesus truly meant that anything asked by His children in His name would be done. We should not attempt to make such an earthshaking statement stand on one text alone, especially since the Lord has told us that "in the mouth of two or three witnesses every word may be established" (Matt. 18:16; cf. 2 Cor. 13:1).

Fortunately, we have more than the required two or three witnesses, and their testimonies are clear and unambiguous. We must have an adamantine foundation to support such a colossal promise. We have such a foundation.

Four times, in unequivocal language, Jesus told us that He or the Father would grant any request that is sent to the Father by His children in His name.

Now add to the statement of Jesus in our text these corroborating statements:

"And whatsoever ye shall ask in my name, that will I do, that the Father may be glorified in the Son" (John 14:13).

"Ye have not chosen me, but I have chosen you, and ordained you, that ye should go and bring forth fruit, and that your fruit should remain: that whatsoever ye shall ask of the Father in my name, he may give it you" (15:16).

"And in that day ye shall ask me nothing. Verily, verily, I say unto you, Whatsoever ye shall ask the Father in my name, he will give it you" (16:23).

Here we have four undeniable statements wherein Jesus promised His followers that He or the Father would give to them anything that they might request in His name.

We have already emphasized the fact—which is common knowledge to all who pray, observe, and think—that Jesus' promise was not based on our attaching His name to our petition. This has not worked for us any better than it worked for the vagabond Jews in Paul's day.

Having established what the meaning of the Master's words is *not*, may we inquire, Just what *is* the meaning of His promise? It is so colossal and made so freely that we cannot wisely shrug our shoulders and pass it by as a meaningless and empty promise. It has great meaning. It has miracle-working power. It was meant to be used. Note that Jesus said that such praying and inevitable answering would glorify "the Father . . . in the Son." Could there be any higher motivation for thus praying? Such must be the motivation of all answerable prayers.

We may come to a better understanding of what it means to ask in another's name by the use of an illustration.

Our government has ambassadors representing us at many courts throughout the world. These ambassadors are men commissioned by our government to speak for us in our name. They bear certain credentials.

In addition to being commissioned by our government to represent us, they must be informed as to the message that our government desires them to communicate for us. The ambassador does not cloister himself for a few days or weeks and prepare a message of his own choosing to convey to the distant court. If he is to speak in our name, he must know the message that we desire him to deliver; he must be authorized to deliver it; and he must not alter the message. If he does, he is not speaking in our name.

Suppose that I should go to the government of England and pose as such an ambassador, professing to be speaking in the name of the United States government; would that make it so? I could meet no requirement as a spokesman, speaking in the name of our government. Regardless of what I said, my words would be empty and my message unheeded.

It is hardly conceivable that I could get audience with any crowned monarch with my fake credentials and my profession that I was speaking in the name of this government; but even if possible, this government could not be bound by such quackery.

To ask in Christ's name is nothing more nor less than to ask at His instigation. Our qualifications are much like those of an earthly ambassador to another court. We must have standing with the Master. We must be informed by Him as to what to say. We must be authorized to impart the message.

It is no strain on the faith of one who believes in the Sonship of Jesus Christ to believe that the Father will listen to what the Son has to say. But what about the ambassador, or the prayer? That need not be a handicap. It is not primarily the rank of the courier; the important factor is the standing of the one who sent the message. No one of higher rank could be speaking, if Christ is the Author of the message.

This is not an oversimplification of the matter. It is just that simple. The prayers thus indited are answered in toto. This is the unmistakable word of the Master: "If ye shall ask any thing in my name, I will do it."

When an ambassador from our government speaks our message that he has been authorized to speak, he is our spokesman, his is our voice, his message is our message; and every battleship that sails the sea, and every bomber that cuts the blue, and every patriot that wears our uniform, stands ready to enforce our message if need requires it.

In like manner, when one speaks to the Father the message of the Son, at the Son's instigation and at His time, all the resources of the heavens would be employed if necessary to fulfill the Son's request. The angels would lay aside their harps if need required and, with swords in hand, enter battle against the forces of darkness that attempt to block out

Christ's messenger in his appointed errand. Such a message is not ours but Christ's. All hell cannot annul it. No such prayer goes unanswered, nor is its request unfulfilled.

All of this sounds great indeed. And indeed, it is as grand as it sounds. The secret is worth looking into.

The question now becomes, How does one get the Son's message? How does he become His spokesman?

The first requirement is to strip one's mind of all personal desires. The slate must be wiped clean so that the Master can write His message thereon. If this appears to be surrendering one's rights, the answer is that this is exactly what it is.

Just look at the matter from another angle, and it may become easier to comprehend. Can we get any request through to the Father that is contrary to the Son? The answer to that question is no. Positively no! The Father and the Son are not at variance. One does not contradict the other. If, therefore, only the Son's requests have significance, what danger is there of clearing the slate of our personal desires to permit Him to enter His own? After all our struggling, we must come back to the "Not my will, but thine, be done" (Luke 22:42). Why not begin there and seek to know that will and avoid all the struggling over our own desires? With His aid we can develop a wise asking from an unprejudiced position much better than to build up our own plan and then have to revise it again and again. The architect should be called before the foundation is laid. We should seek to learn the verdict of the Judge before we make the appeal. Christ knows what the verdict is to be and stands ready to help us frame an appeal that will be honored.

This understanding of the prayer life brings us up to the necessity of understanding the will of God. Here we must acquaint ourselves with the living God.

Nowhere do we stand in greater need of the help of the Spirit than in our prayer life. All of true religion centers in

38

life—the life of the living God. Our prayers are lifeless until activated by the Spirit. This is what is meant by praying in the Holy Ghost. Such prayers are answered.

Answered prayers are limited to those sponsored by the Spirit or at least sanctioned by Him. For the Spirit to oppose our petition is for the petition to go unanswered. God will not do anything contrary to His own will, and the Son will not indite a petition through us that is not in harmony with the divine will. In all of His earthly life Jesus refused to ask for himself anything that would not meet with the approval of the Father, and we may rest assured that He will not begin to do so for us. Our first task is to get into line with the thought of the Master, then let our requests be made known.

Admittedly this is a high plateau of prayer, but no higher than the promised answer. One cannot expect to secure a diamond for a song. The prize is worth the searching. The winner will be overjoyed and fully satisfied. God, too, will be happy, for such asking and receiving honors the Father. He is "glorified in the Son" when we thus pray.

Let us get acquainted with the Master, so that we may more often ask in His name and thus honor both the Father and the Son, and have our own joy fulfilled.

I Might Save Some

(Rom. 11:14)

In Paul's letter to the Romans he wrote, "If by any means I . . . might save some of them" (Rom. 11:14). To the Corinthians he expressed the same thing, saying, "I am made all things to all men, that I might by all means save some" (1 Cor. 9:22).

No one who is acquainted with the ministry and teaching of the great apostle could accuse him of neglecting any means of soul winning. So earnest was he in his efforts to reach his kinsmen that he said, "I could wish that myself were accursed from Christ for my brethren" (Rom. 9:3). He stood ready to use any means for men's salvation. Note the expressions in the above passages: "I am made all things to all men"; "if by any means"; "by all means." He threw into the effort of soul winning every known means of salvation: prayer, fasting, preaching, and even offering his life for their souls.

No one can deny that he knew the worth of these means. He knew prevailing prayer and its worth, along with the value of other means; but it is to be noted that having employed "all means," "any means," "all things," and life itself, he hoped to save only "some." In other words, with one deft blow he struck death to the misconception that the intercessor can pray the final prayer, speak the final word for the soul of another. If this mighty weapon, so effectively wielded by the apostle, could be decisive, he could not refer to saving "some." He would save all for whom he prayed.

By these words we do not minimize the power of prayer for the lost. Its power is great and its full potential unused; all we are merely pointing out is the fallacy that it is final. This Paul unmistakably affirms.

Some honest but misguided saints have assumed the finality of prayer for a lost son or daughter, throwing their souls and faith into the effort to make it real, and then have failed and have wrecked their faith.

Two undeniable things should be impressed indelibly upon our minds: (1) Prayer for the lost is powerful but not final; (2) after all that one can do for the lost, only some will be reached.

Error in one's belief at this point is not damaging until acted upon; then it could be disastrous. When one enters the field of intercession, he should know that he could fail.

It is not reasonable to believe that our intercession is more availing than that of Christ and the Holy Spirit. We can enter with them into this sacred ministry, but we can never excel them. The record is that the Holy Spirit is making intercession for us with unutterable groanings. We are also told that Jesus is at the Father's right hand, praying for us. Whose prayers could be more valuable and availing than theirs? But theirs are not final, else we could not be lost; but we may fail, their prayers notwithstanding.

Prayers for souls is relative but not final. It may be likened to the ministry of the doctor and the nurse. Such ministry is effective but not final. Many sick would die but for their ministry, and yet health cannot be guaranteed by the best medical methods. In like manner, many souls may be lost without our prayers; although powerful, they can't assure a sinner's salvation.

To assume that the final destiny of the lost rests ultimately upon the Christian and Christ would be to make the sinners' eternal doom unjust. The neglectful saint should bear it.

41

To pursue this line of false claim to the end, one must make God and the angels responsible for the problem of sin in the universe. Did Christ not intercede for the angels? If not, why not? And if He did, they could not have fallen if His prayer had been final.

Neither God the Father nor the Son will bear the burden of man's fallen estate, and the Christian, however neglectful, cannot bear it fully. The sinner, who carries the final vote, must bear justly the doom of his own eternal death.

Great, and in many cases eternal, harm has been done by earnest Christians who have claimed to have had assurance that some loved one—usually a member of the family—would be saved at last. Such a claim, when known and believed by the one thus prayed for, often immunizes such an one against the gospel and gives him a false security from which he may never awaken. The deceived intercessor may live to know that his belief was false and may give up faith completely.

To further complicate the matter and make the error more dangerous is the fact that cases can be cited where such intercessory prayer had been offered, such claim of the assurance announced, and the prayed-for results achieved. To the uninformed and unthinking this is proof enough; but for one who seeks final truth, there must be laid beside such claims the other equally documented claims that did not materialize.

A very common parallel of belief may be found in another case. Some believe (and I have such a friend) that if a black cat runs across the road in front of your moving car, it is an omen of bad luck. This friend, although a college graduate and a Bible teacher in the church, insists on the driver circling the block to avert the bad luck.

When the matter is discussed with her, she brings up case after case—so well established that no one could deny—to prove her point. The instances cited are, without reasonable doubt, true; but it is also true—and as well proven—that there are many more black cat crossings that bring no bad luck. Yet the belief persists.

One cannot always conclude that when an object is prayed for and received, it came as an answer to prayer. In this country, one may pray for months for rain, and rain will come. It always has during my lifetime, but it could be folly to claim that the rain came in answer to prayer. Even if one cursed for the same length of time, rain would come. In none of these cases does the exception establish the rule.

How Often Would I

(Luke 13:34)

The "How Often Would I" of our theme reveals the intense and repeated interest Jesus had for Jerusalem in His day. It is more fully expressed in these words: "And when he was come near, he beheld the city, and wept over it" (Luke 19:41).

This weeping over Jerusalem was not an isolated instance. It was but one of the "often" weepings referred to in our theme. Back of these tears were His teachings, preaching, and praying in the city. No one can question His love and interest for this capital city, nor can anyone accuse Him of doing less that His all to save it; and yet He was compelled to pronounce its doom: "Behold, your house is left unto you desolate" (Luke 13:35).

The story not only portrays the interest of the Master in the salvation of the city, but deeper still, it reveals the inability of even the Son of God to turn the hearts of men to God without their consent.

There have been those among us who have claimed too much for the intercession of Christ and His followers on the behalf of the unsaved. This weeping of the Savior and His subsequent announcement of the city's doom illustrates His helplessness to speak the final word for a city or any one of its citizens.

Christ at Jerusalem illustrates the role of the Christian in a sinful world. There should be tears of intercession for the lost and, at the same time, the knowledge that the subject of

44

our tears and prayers has the final word. To fail to see this is to lay a foundation for the wreckage of one's faith.

In our effort to follow Christ ourselves and to encourage others to do so, we encounter two problems—first, that of not having enough interest to produce tears. Christ wept over the sin of Jerusalem. He wept bitterly and often. To be Christ-like, we must share that attitude for the sinning of our day. We certainly need help at this point.

The second problem we face is the false assumption that our tears and prayers always will be effective and final for those for whom we weep and pray. This is not a problem of the disinterested, but it has at times become a problem to the intercessor.

Without doubt, professed followers of Christ should be aroused to tears and prayers for the lost. There is a dearth of interest in this area; but having thus aroused them, we should guard them against the second danger of claiming too much in response to their prayers and tears. Here the instance of Christ and Jerusalem helps us.

There are many religious leaders urging prayer for the lost, yet saying little of the possibility of assuming that our interest in the unsaved can do more than is possible. For this reason, we are sounding the warning that the one for whom intercession is being made has the final word, and not the intercessor. This is evident from the lesson of Christ and Jerusalem that is before us.

Intercessory prayer for the lost, whether made by Jesus, the Holy Spirit, or by the saints, is powerful and effective in only a limited way, and not in an absolute one. Such prayer may cause God to extend mercy to the one interceded for; it may bring across his path other messengers to warn him; it may cause him to see more plainly the condition of his soul and the path to God.

The weeping of Jesus over Jerusalem was often, and there is value and possible success in these additional weep-

45

ings and prayers; but the final decision rests not with the pray-er but with the one for whom prayer is made.

This is clearly seen in the incident before us and is further illustrated by the fact that Jesus, the great Intercessor, is making intercession for us, and yet in spite of it, we could be lost—else all who were prayed for could not be lost. The "falling away" is taught in the Word (2 Thess. 2:3) as well as the intercession of Christ; hence, His intercession is not final.

To make the intercessor responsible for the sinner is to place the blame of the soul's lostness upon the saint and the interceding Christ, and not upon the sinner. The saint's tears and prayers are helpful and at times are the very help that the sinner needs to help him to the Savior; the danger is the belief that it *always* may be so. Let prayer be useful and powerful, but relative and not absolute, and it can remain a useful instrument in men's salvation; but even it cannot always prevail.

Should one reading these lines be of the opinion that Christ, the Holy Spirit, and the holy, by tears and intercession, can guarantee the salvation of others, let him answer this question: How, then, the fall of Lucifer and the angels? We are told that the "angels . . . kept not their first estate" but fell (Jude 6). Were the Holy Spirit and Christ dilatory in their intercession, as mortals are prone to be?

If Christ's intercession can guarantee the ultimate salvation of the Christian, why could it not have kept the angels from falling? Surely no one would charge Christ with failing them, nor would anyone charge Him with doing more for us than for the angels. He made both angels and man, and surely He had as much interest in keeping the inhabitants of heaven holy as He has in keeping Christians of earth ready for heaven.

The solemn fact remains that God has made man a free moral agent who can, as Stephen said, "always resist the Holy Ghost" (Acts 7:51). Man, not God, speaks the final word

46

as to his eternal destiny; hence, Christ is represented as standing at the door outside, knocking, and His entry depends upon the occupant hearing His voice and opening the door.

His weeping over Jerusalem often and then announcing the fate of the city, bespeaks His love but helplessness to save without man's consent.

God Is Not Governed by His Power

God is not in bondage to His own power. He does not do all that He is capable of doing. He uses His power, but He is not ruled by it. He is guided by His wisdom, and His use of His power is determined by this wisdom.

These statements are self-evident to one who thinks. God has power to blot man off the earth; He did this once and has not lost the power to do so again. He destroyed cities and wicked men in the past and retains that power. The use of His power is not determined by its presence but by His infinite wisdom.

He saved Daniel from the lions, He healed the blind and the leper, He raised the dead, and He stilled the storm in the past. His power is the same, so we feel that He should use His power in our behalf.

It is normal for man in distress to appeal to the power of God for deliverance. With a son on active duty overseas in wartime, we may have prayed, "Lord, You have the power to protect my boy from danger and death." In sickness, we pray, "Lord, You can heal my child; You have that power to heal, and we ask You to do so."

In such cases, we are asking God to exercise His power according to our desire. It seems to us that to spare the life of the son in war, and raise the child from the deathbed, is the proper thing to do, so we insist that God exercise His power to that end.

We know that power can only be exercised by someone who has it, and the exercising thereof is determined by the person who possesses it. The will and wisdom of its possessor, and not the will and wisdom of the petitioner, is the determining factor. Therefore the basis for the exercise of the divine power lies in God's will and not ours. All of our petitions will be fruitless until they pass from the area of our choosing into the area of His wisdom.

We should not condemn ourselves for appealing first to the power of God. It seems so sensible. We have the need, and He has the power to meet that need. It seems good to us; in fact, it appears to us to be the best thing to do. Would He not see eye to eye with us? It seems that He should; hence we ask Him to exercise His power according to our seeing.

We repeat, one should not condemn himself for thus asking and acting. It is according to one's best judgment. We are further justified in presenting to God our best judgment, for the Master followed this same path; He was "made like unto his brethren" (Heb. 2:17), and He too made His first appeal to God's power when in a crisis.

More than two instances of such are of record. We shall use only two. In Gethsemane, He prayed, "Abba, Father, all things are possible unto thee; take away this cup from me: nevertheless not what I will, but what thou wilt" (Mark 14:36). Here He first appeals to the power of the Father but yields to the will of the Father; however, God chose not to use His power, and the cup was not taken away.

Again it is said of Him, "When he had offered up prayers and supplications with strong crying and tears unto him that was able to save him from death, [He] was heard in that he feared" (Heb. 5:7). Here again He appealed to the Father's power at first but put the Father's will ahead of His desire; so He "was heard" but not saved from death.

This passing from our will, based upon what we think to be best, to His will, which is best, is, at times, a painful process. At times we feel so sure that our way is best that we are reluctant to surrender; we are so sure our way is right. This struggle does not invalidate our consecration. If we have settled it to go God's way, we will find it—although it may be "with strong crying and tears." That was true of the Master.

This obedience to the Father, which was Christ's avowed and unaltered purpose, must be learned; and "though he were a Son, yet learned he obedience by the things which he suffered" (Heb. 5:8).

One may come to Him in all honesty, knowing that He has power to grant our request, and with equal honesty of belief that our asking is in His will; but one must remember that His ways are above our ways as truly as the heavens are above the earth. We must, therefore, say in the end, "Thy will be done." There is no other way, for life begins with surrender. It was true in Christ's case and must be in ours.

We cannot cling to His power as a basis for the answer. His wisdom controls its use, and we cannot fathom His wisdom; hence the necessity of surrendering our will and wisdom and seeking to find His, that we may be guided by it.

To press our petition, assuming that it is right and best, is to place our will above His, and that is sin—a sin that the Son would not commit; and if we do, our prayers will go unheeded.

Someone may say, Then why pray? The answer is that we pray so as to enter into the mind and thought of God and unite our prayer with His will. This is "praying in the Holy Ghost" (Jude 20)—being united with God in our asking.

This is nothing more nor less than a surrender of our plan and will to Him. This was the unchanged purpose of the Master, and to be like Him, ours must be the same.

Let us turn for a moment from the Scriptures and use our common sense. Do you honestly believe that your will and way are better than His? If you really believe that His way is best, why would you hesitate to relinquish your will for His?

50

Jesus did this and taught us to do so also. If we refuse to say in truth, "Not my will, but thine, be done" (Luke 22:42), we are elevating ourselves above our Maker. It matters not how it may seem to us, the indisputable fact is that God's way is the best for us, as well as for Him and His cause.

The driving force of our praying should be, "Thy kingdom come. Thy will be done in earth, as it is [done] in heaven" (Matt. 6:10)—perfectly. This is what Jesus taught, and He is right.

Surrender—absolute, complete, eternal surrender—of ourselves, our wills, our loves, our hearts, our all to the Master is the only condition that will make heaven possible for us.

This surrender must be made in the face of possible rejection of every member of our family, every friend, and every church, and life itself. To willfully hold back any part of what we are or what we have is to be cut off from Him. God killed two at the altar of the Early Church who held back only "part of the price" but claimed that they had paid it all (Acts 5:1-11).

In the light of this demand, one may more easily understand the Master's words, "Many will say to me in that day, Lord, Lord . . . and then will I profess unto them, I never knew you: depart from me" (Matt. 7:22-23).

We can know when our surrender is complete: We will have peace, rest, and a presence—the presence of the Holy Spirit. Cast your prayer in with the intercession of Christ and the Holy Spirit. They pray in the Father's will, and the Father hears them.

Men Ought Always to Pray

If I were to place above the door to my prayer closet a rule that should guide my prayer life from Christian infancy to the end of life's journey, it would be "Men ought always to pray" (Luke 18:1).

Note first, that this is a divine command, and there is no way to deal with a divine command but to obey it; and if one is not willing to obey it, he need not enter the prayer closet. There is only one law for the Kingdom, and that is obedience. This was the Master's set purpose, and His children can have no other.

Obedience to this principle will cause everyone to triumph over every discouraging situation, and there are many. We shall name only a few.

First: The seeming futility of prayer. One may pray repeatedly for what he thinks he should have and what he sincerely believes to be God's will for him, but no answer comes. Then the question arises, Why pray? The answer is written above the prayer closet door: "Men ought always to pray."

Second: The sense of utter ignorance as to knowing how to pray, and what to pray for. Although the Scriptures clearly tell us that is the case, nevertheless one may grow weary with an ignorance that seems never to vanish. Our knowing the how and the what of prayer are not necessary; our duty is clearly marked: "Men ought always to pray."

Third: The apparent waste of time spent in prayers that produce no visible results (and the central request in the prayer taught by Jesus has been prayed for almost 2,000 years and has not been answered). If we are obedient, we will append our petition to the long list; and unless He comes soon, it will not be answered in our lifetime. The prayer request is that "Thy will be done in earth, as it is in heaven" (Matt. 6:10). God has promised a day when "the earth shall be full of the knowledge of the Lord, as the waters cover the sea" (Isa. 11:9). For that day we pray, and it will come someday. The problems that these facts present are all duly answered in our theme: "Men ought always to pray."

Fourth: The multitudinous duties that press in upon us. The other work for God. The ministries to the needy. The assignments of the church. The cries for help. In short, the good things that consume our time. Surely God will understand that while we would like very much to take time to pray, we haven't time to do so. The answer remains the same; nothing can justly become a substitute for obedience. "Men ought always to pray."

Fifth: The substitute of the belief in obedience to this divinely enjoined rule for obedience itself. James tells us that "faith without works is dead" (2:20, 26); and Jesus closed the Sermon on the Mount by saying that it was not enough to hear His words, but only the one who did what He said could stand in the last reckoning day.

Sixth: Just plain weariness. And that danger is called to attention following the words of my theme: "And not to faint." These words say two things: They remind us that fainting is a danger ever facing the one who would pray, but they also tell us that prayer will prevent the fainting.

There are many incentives for praying set forth in God's Word, many benefits to us and those for whom we pray, and wonderful fellowship with the Spirit who prays with us. But when the glory of the prayer time fades, the joy of aloneness

53

with Him seeps away, and the "cares of this life" consume our time (Luke 21:34), it is then that sheer duty, like an iron hand, comes to center and says, Regardless of how you feel, how much you have to do, how little your prayers avail, the fact remains: "Men ought always to pray."

There are many reasons why one "ought . . . to pray," and I would put at the top of the list companionship with Christ. "He ever liveth to make intercession" for us (Heb. 7:25), and to enter into the labors of the Master is the highest privilege known to man. It also enters into partnership with the Holy Spirit who "maketh intercession . . . with groanings which cannot be uttered" (Rom. 8:26).

Praying unites the pray-ers; it puts them on familiar ground. It blends their spirits. It is the cement that holds the Body of Christ together.

Then, too, there is a glorious value to the prayers of the saints that we will never know until we see its revelation in the final days. Then the prayers of the saint will be poured out in the presence of God and will arise as enjoyable incense to Him. While we cannot understand all that means, be assured that nothing but the highly prized will be presented on that glorious day. Let us keep the message over the portal ever before us: "Men ought always to pray"!

Prayer at Its Best

The Bible contains the record of many prayers, prayers for many and varied things—things personal, things temporal, and things eternal; but I can think of no human prayer that is deeper than the apostle Paul prayed: "That I may know him, and the power of his resurrection, and the fellowship of his sufferings, being made conformable unto his death" (Phil. 3:10).

A person may have fellowship with another at different levels. A man told me that he and his wife got on well until it came to politics, and that became such a battleground that they agreed never to make politics a subject of discussion. Some are great cronies in sports but part company when it comes to religion. Jesus described human love at its depth as being willing to die for a friend. When one shares that kind of love with a friend, he is sharing at the human depth.

Likewise, there are depths in Christ, and one may share with Him on some levels and never explore the deeper levels of His nature. The deepest love of Christ was exemplified when He willingly died for His enemies. We have no record that Stephen, the first Christian martyr, voluntarily gave his life for his enemies, but we do know that he followed the pattern of the Crucified in asking, "Lord, lay not this sin to their charge" (Acts 7:60).

The apostle Paul had a deep love when he said, "I could wish that myself were accursed from Christ for my brethren, my kinsmen according to the flesh" (Rom. 9:3). Note, he was not speaking of the Gentiles nor his enemies, but kinfolk.

Love here could have been human, and certainly it was not the type that Jesus had for His enemies.

Paul was praying for a depth of knowledge of Christ that he did not have, else his prayer is meaningless. He had met Christ on the Damascus road, so he knew Him, but not deeply and fully. He later said, "I know whom I have believed" (2 Tim. 1:12). Yes, Paul knew Him. He never doubted that nor hesitated to confess it; but here he was reaching for a deeper depth, a depth of fellowship in suffering, a oneness with Christ at His depth.

At first reading it appears that the requests of the text are out of sequence. The verse opens with an expression of the apostle's deep desire: "That I may know him." In the eighth verse, he tells us the extent to which that desire ran: "I count all things but loss for the excellency of the knowledge of Christ Jesus my Lord: for whom I have suffered the loss of all things, and do count them but dung, that I may win Christ."

He knew Christ in saving power. He knew the Holy Spirit as a director of his life, but he is reaching out for a fuller knowledge of his Lord, a deeper union with Him. In the two following requests, it would seem illogical for him to ask for "the power of his resurrection" and then "the fellowship of his sufferings"; that would seem to be an anticlimax, but not so, for the suffering that he was reaching for was to come from witnessing the power of His resurrection—a post-Resurrection suffering.

The resurrection he refers to is not the final resurrection of the body but the spiritual resurrection that he had referred to when "God ... raised us up together, and made us sit together in heavenly places in Christ Jesus" (Eph. 2:4, 6). The Ephesians to whom he wrote this letter had been saved and subsequently filled with the Holy Spirit (1:13), but they were still blind to all that was involved in "the exceeding greatness of his power to us-ward" (v. 19).

The requests are in the proper order, for it is only after

one has been resurrected into this heavenly relationship that he can begin to fellowship with Christ in His deeper sufferings. Paul had the suffering for his kinfolk, reaching even to a desire to die for them. Knowing that Christ's love led to suffering even unto death for His enemies, he seems to be reaching out for this maximum love. For this he was praying: to have fellowship with Christ in His deepest suffering—death for His enemies. When one is thus praying, prayer is at its best.

At the cost of convicting myself, I am faced with three undeniable facts:

1. "The Spirit itself maketh intercession for us with groanings which cannot be uttered" (Rom. 8:26).

2. "He [Jesus] is able . . . to save . . . seeing he ever liveth to make intercession for them" (Heb. 7:25).

3. "I exhort therefore, that, first of all, supplications, prayers, intercessions . . . be made for all men" (1 Tim. 2:1).

Can we be one with Christ, in the fullest sense, without sharing His constant labors? Can we be truly filled with the Spirit and have no soul-moving concern for the lost? Can we be fully obedient to God and heed not His exhortation to us in this regard? There is but one answer.

We all want to reign with Jesus, but that honor is reserved only for those who "suffer" with Him (2 Tim. 2:12). Do you desire to be "glad . . . with exceeding joy" when His glory is revealed? This joy is promised to those who are "partakers of Christ's sufferings" (1 Pet. 4:13). Do you desire to be among the "heirs of God, and joint-heirs with Christ . . . [and] be also glorified together"? If so, this is promised, "if so be that we suffer with him" (Rom. 8:17). "For unto you it is given in the behalf of Christ, not only to believe on him, but also to suffer for his sake" (Phil. 1:29).

What greater, deeper, and more rewarding suffering could one enter into than into the intercession of the resurrected Christ and the blessed Holy Spirit?

Our church lays great emphasis upon God's call unto holiness, and rightly so. There is a call to suffering equally clear: "For even hereunto were ye called: because Christ also suffered for us, leaving us an example, that ye should follow his steps" (1 Pet. 2:21).

The prayer of intercession to the point of pain is "Prayer at Its Best."

God, You Do the Talking

So often we consume our quiet hour—if such we have—telling God what we want and when we want it, with little thought of why we want it or what we want it for. This may explain the paucity of our receipts. James has a word at this point: "Ye ask, and receive not, because ye ask amiss, that ye may consume it upon your lusts" (James 4:3). The passion of the soul is self-interest, and the motive in the asking is self-enjoyment.

In the light of the fact that what we say to God is secondary and His message to us is primary, it is time for us to say, "Now, God, You do the talking, and I will listen."

Centuries ago, a mere lad requested God to do the talking, and God did. Not only did the lad request the speaking, but he promised to listen. This is the indispensable prerequisite to communion with the Divine.

Samuel had heard the words "Samuel, Samuel" three times. The words were clear; they were the words of a man, so he thought. They were not vague, strange, or of another tongue. "It is Eli calling," he said to himself and answered the call. "Now Samuel did not yet know the Lord" (1 Sam. 3:7), but he was advised by Eli that it was the Lord; so when he heard again the familiar call, "Samuel, Samuel," he gave an answer that became the guiding rule of his long and useful life: "Speak, Lord; for thy servant heareth." In other words, he was saying, "Lord, You do the taking, and I will listen and obey."

Significantly, it is recorded that "the word of the Lord

was precious in those days" (v. 1). The margin expresses it, "The word was rare . . . no frequent or widespread vision."

When it is said that the Word of the Lord was "rare in those days," the reference was not made to the written law that God had given to them through Moses, but rather to the current speaking of God concerning things needful for them but that were not spelled out in the written law.

The message delivered to Samuel was personal for Eli and was no part of God's written law. This need for a speaking voice is told over and over again in the Word. It is not at variance with the written Word but rather provided for in the Word of the law. Here is a clear case of such provision: "Thou hast avouched the Lord this day to be thy God, and to walk in his ways, and to keep his statutes, and his commandments, and his judgments, and to hearken unto his voice" (Deut. 26:17).

Although the law of Moses had been fully written, the Voice had not been silenced, nor has it been silenced since.

It is folly for us to pray as did Samuel: "Speak; for thy servant heareth," if there be no speaking God. The facts are, He has spoken through ages past and would speak to us today, if we have ears to hear, which means if we have the mind to obey.

This art of listening is illustrated in the life of the Master while upon earth. He said, "As I hear, I judge"; and again, "I speak therefore, even as the Father said unto me, so I speak" (John 5:30; 12:50). Thus speaking, He was not referring to the written Word, with which He was familiar and which He often quoted, but to the spoken messages that He was often receiving from the Father. Jesus Christ was first a listener and then a speaker, and what He spoke grew out of what He heard. "I do nothing of myself; but as my Father hath taught me, I speak these things" (8:28).

It is interesting to note that the Holy Spirit walked the same path as the listening Christ. Of Him it was said, "Whatsoever he shall hear, that shall he speak" (John 16:13). He originated no business but was a conveyor of the Father's message. He was first a listener and then a speaker.

This listening, then speaking, pattern followed by the Son and the Spirit was the pattern given to the prophets of old. The command to them was, "Thou shalt hear the word at my mouth, and warn them from me" (Ezek. 33:7). Following this advice, Balaam said to Balak, "I cannot go beyond the word of the Lord my God, to do less or more" (Num. 22:18). True to the divine pattern, the fearless Micaiah spoke the message of God to King Ahab: "As the Lord liveth, what the Lord saith unto me, that will I speak" (1 Kings 22:14).

What was required of God's messengers in Old Testament days is required of the would-be messengers of Christ today. The record is clear: "If any man speak, let him speak as the oracles of God" (1 Pet. 4:11). The command is a universal one: "If any man speak." There is no place in God's ministry for a message of uncertainty: "For if the trumpet give an uncertain sound, who shall prepare himself to the battle?" (1 Cor. 14:8).

There is no finality except in the Word of God. Jesus spoke "as one having authority" (Matt. 7:29), because He spoke the Word of God. A very lamentable fact concerning much of today's preaching is its lack of finality. Often it is the "best thinking of the Arminian school," or "the Calvinist school," or "Protestantism," or "Catholicism," by which alone no honest soul can be bound. The mind must pierce beneath the creeds of men and draw its life from the spring of God's eternal Word revealed by the Teacher Christ sent to reveal it to us. Nothing short of a Spirit-revealed Word can satisfy the human soul. This is not to say that others have not found the same and declared it, but it is to say their declaration of what they have come to know cannot be ground for our final faith. The message from the Master to would-be followers was, "Come and see" (John 1:39); and it still echoes through the ages. This is a personal message and must have our personal response.

Every honest soul who, like young Samuel of old, asks God to speak and pledges obedience to the message will hear the Master's voice and will be shown the right path. This is the path of the divine messengers who spoke with authority; and it is the only path of the Master who could say, "I do always those things that please him" (John 8:29); the path of the Spirit who searches and listens and then speaks the Father's word; the path of the divine messengers who spoke with authority; and it is the only path of worth for you and for me. "Speak, Lord; for thy servant heareth."

Angels Have It Hard, Too

This "holy war," as John Bunyan called it, is but dimly understood by mortal man. At what point in the timeless past it began, and when in time to come it will end, is known only to God. This much we do know: It is in progress now, we are involved in it, and our eternal destiny hinges on how we "fight the good fight of faith" and "endure unto the end" (1 Tim. 6:12; Matt. 24:13).

This war is rightly called a "holy war," for it was begun on earth by God. He is the One who said to the serpent in the Garden of Eden, "I will put enmity between thee and the woman, and between thy seed and her seed"; and when thus speaking God also announced the outcome: "It shall bruise thy head, and thou shalt bruise his heel" (Gen. 3:15).

This "holy war," announced in Eden, may well be viewed against the background of what might well be called the "unholy" war—the one begun in the heavenlies by Lucifer, who arose in insurrection against God. We assume that this war or insurrection was quickly ended. "The angels which kept not their first estate, . . . he hath reserved in everlasting chains under darkness unto the judgment of the great day" (Jude 6). Peter confirms the testimony of Jude by saying, "God spared not the angels that sinned" (2 Pet. 2:4).

The war, started by God in Eden to wrest from Satan all possible souls, has been a long conflict. It will come to a victorious end for God; but in the meantime, the fighting has been fierce upon earth. "We wrestle not against flesh and blood, but against principalities, against powers, against the rulers of the darkness of this world, against spiritual wickedness in high places" (Eph. 6:12). Every Christian is engaged in this warfare, and the closer he lives to the Master the more severe the battles will be. No one knew the power of the evil one as did Christ, and Christlikeness means encounters with Satan.

Not only are the children of God engaged in this warfare, but so are the angels of God. Of the last days we read, "There was war in heaven: Michael and his angels fought against the dragon; and the dragon fought and his angels" (Rev. 12:7).

This holy war has been carried on in terrible conflict. The suffering of Christ gives insight, the death of the martyrs gives proof, but the heavens are engaged also. The intercession of Christ and the groaning of the Holy Spirit make this perfectly clear; but it is to the struggles of the angels that we wish to draw attention. The encounter of Michael the archangel with the devil gives some insight. Michael had respect for the power of the devil and did not rail at him, but said, "The Lord rebuke thee" (Jude 9).

The fullest and most penetrating insight given to us concerning the difficulty confronting the angels in executing the divine commands is found in the Book of Daniel. This is very illuminating, because it is set forth so graphically. It is a rather shocking account, since it shows the hard and prolonged struggle of the angel, and the final necessity of securing additional angelic assistance. The incident is more shocking since the general conception appears to be that angels go as they are sent and are amply able to do all they are asked to do without struggle or delay. This insight into the struggle of the heavenly messenger with the prince of Media is therefore very illuminating and could well be typical of the problems that the angels have in carrying on their work.

Daniel, residing in the Medo-Persian Empire, and desiring information from God concerning a vision that had been given him, "was mourning three full weeks. I ate no pleasant bread [he said], neither came flesh nor wine in my mouth . . . till three whole weeks were fulfilled" (Dan. 10:2-3).

Then comes the heavenly messenger with this startling revelation: "From the first day that thou didst set thine heart to understand, . . . thy words were heard . . . But the prince of the kingdom of Persia withstood me one and twenty days: but, lo, Michael, one of the chief princes, came to help me" (Dan. 10:12-13). This prince of Media, who withstood the messenger for three weeks, was not an earthly prince but a satanic prince referred to in Paul's letter to the Ephesians. This prince ruled over a satanic principality that ruled over the Medo-Persian Empire in which Daniel was living. Paul tells us here is where we fight, and note that the fighting is on both sides of this satanic principality, located in the heavens between us and God. Beneath it was faithful Daniel, bombarding the skies in fasting and in prayer; and above it, a messenger of God trying to break through. The battle raged for three long weeks, and help from God was brought in; Michael came to aid, and a breakthrough came.

Here is clearly seen the struggles of the angelic host as it presses against the forces of the "god of this world" (2 Cor. 4:4). Angels have their struggles, too.

More than one lesson emerges from the incident. First, the need of perseverance in prayer. Here was a prayer heard on the first day it started, but not answered until the 21st —strange but true. Some of our ideas about our easy-going, nonproductive praying need to be changed. Wrestling and agony, such as Christ's in the garden, is not alone for Him; nor is it the Holy Spirit alone who must make intercession "with groanings which cannot be uttered" (Rom. 8:26). If there are to be victories, there must be warfare.

The story contains this encouraging revelation. There are more angels in heaven, and in a tight place another will be sent. No angelic defeat is of record; delay, but ultimate victory.

In contemplating this incident, a disturbing thought comes to my mind. From the record we learn that Daniel initiated the warfare, and the coming of the angel was in answer to his prayer. That much we know. The angel's words are, "Thy words were heard, and I am come for thy words" (Dan. 10:12).

The question is this: If the angel's effort was caused by Daniel's prayer, would the angel continue his effort if Daniel ceased his? In this case, the angel was the helper. Would the helper continue when there was no one seeking help?

The least we can say of this is, there is need of persistence. This is taught clearly by Christ elsewhere.

Hurrah for the angels! They are warriors who fight against odds, but get through alone or by the assistance of others.

Thunder, Angel, or God?

(John 12:29)

What was it? Thunder, angel, or God? It was an audible sound; they all heard it. It was not an inward impression that came to the Master; others could not have heard that, but they heard. They had "ears to hear," but they heard not.

The noise, though inarticulate, was useful, for Jesus said that it "came . . . for your sakes." There is a certain beneficial effect of God's speaking, whether men fully understand it or not. The supernatural movements of the Spirit create a sense of the divine that is wholesome.

The purpose of the "thunder" must have been to create a sense of awe in the presence of Christ, for it is evident that those who heard it connected it in some way with Christ; and the fact that the heavens recognized Him would create a sense of respect for Him and mark Him as one with a heavenly connection.

It is not clear whether their spiritual deafness was due to their distance from God, or that God did not desire them to understand. He has, at other times, closed the ears of people, and this may have been another such instance. Whatever our answer, it did have a purpose, and that purpose was fulfilled.

There was another class of hearers there. They detected more than thunder. They sensed that there was a message in the noise, but they heard it not. It could be that they had no belief that a heavenly voice could be understandable. For them it was an omen, a signal of uncertain meaning. It had meaning, but of its meaning they could not be certain.

To Christ it was a clear-cut message, understandable, and meaningful; and in it we see His vital, conscious, and repeated contact with the Father. The voice from the skies to Him was always understandable. He had at times, like ourselves, to weed out the voice of the imitator, but in the end the voice of the Father was always clear.

This instance is but one in the life of Jesus when the Voice came in clarity and distinctness. There were others equally clear. These experiences were not peculiar to the Son alone, nor is it God's plan that there be no more. The record is replete with the speaking of God to men. God spoke to Moses, to Abraham, to Joseph, to Peter, to Paul, to John, and to many others.

There is nothing that can prove that one is alive better than the demonstration that he can speak. We are warned not to "depart . . . from the living God" (Heb. 3:12), the God who proves that He is alive by His speaking—*now*, and not only in the past.

That Jesus expected us to have a spoken word from heaven in our day is clearly seen in the announced work of the Holy Spirit. He has asked us to receive the Holy Spirit, and He said of Him: "Whatsoever he shall hear, that shall he speak" (John 16:13). He is a speaking Spirit and is commissioned to do so, but it is one thing to have a speaker, and it is another thing to hear what He says. Could it be that we are so far removed from Christ that His voice is but that of an angel and unintelligible at that? Or worse still, does it come to us as mere thunder?

When has the Spirit said anything to you that you knew to be the voice of God? Was it clear, distinct, understandable, and certainly God's? From my conversations with many professed Christians over long years, I am fully persuaded, based upon their statements and not on my opinions, that there is but little of the Voice heard by us.

Has God changed His plan? Would He no longer speak? Do we need Him no more? Just what is the problem? If we can charge it off to the fact that He has changed His plan—written a Book and gone into silence—then we are innocent. If, on the other hand, we have become so deafened by the din of things that His voice is but thunder, that is something else.

"My sheep hear my voice," Jesus said in John 10:27. One will readily admit that if He does still speak and it is possible for us to hear, then nothing could be greater than to understand and heed His voice.

Every Bible reference to His speaking indicates that He would still speak if we care to hear.

Let us examine our own hearts to see if we are meeting the conditions on which He reveals himself. One of old wrote, "As the hart panteth after the water brooks, so panteth my soul after thee, O God" (Ps. 42:1). Can my reader honestly say that his soul is thus panting? Again the Psalmist declares, "Mine eyes prevent the night watches, that I might meditate in thy word"; and "with my whole heart have I sought thee" (119:148, 10).

The wise man said, "If thou seekest her as silver, and searchest for her as for hid treasures; then shalt thou understand" (Prov. 2:4-5).

Who among us hungers, thirsts, and seeks as these passages indicate? These are the conditions, and if we have not met them, why deny that God would reveal himself to us if we thus lived?

To Jesus, the Voice was not thunder nor an angel, it was that of His own Father. How did He know, when others were in doubt? Take a look at His life with the Father, and the answer is apparent. He spent hours, and at times even whole nights, alone with Him. He heard His Voice often and came to know it. He met all of the conditions for knowing. He sought His Father's will and presence as more valuable than gold, honor, or any gift of man. To know and to do His will was uppermost in His mind. He listened and obeyed. He exemplified what He preached to us: "If any man will do his will, he shall know" (John 7:17). He obtained the knowledge of the Father by listening to His voice and obeying it.

To me the picture is quite clear. We have become so engrossed in "the cares of this world, and the deceitfulness of riches" (Mark 4:19) that the Voice is no more expected; and when it comes, it sounds like thunder. We can't believe it to be Him, so we go on alone.

Whatsoever He Saith unto You, Do It

(John 2:5)

The theme of this message, "Whatsoever he saith unto you, do it," was spoken by the mother of Jesus to the servants at the wedding in Cana of Galilee and reflects the central responsibility of man to Jesus Christ.

From this simple incident merge some interesting truths. The command given by Jesus to the servants to fill the water-pots with water was a seemingly ordinary command and, when carried out, would be inconsequential. Little did the servants know that they were having a firsthand participation in the opening event of the miraculous career of the Son of God. The part they played seemed so mediocre, and yet it was an essential part of an earthshaking miracle that brought Jesus into the limelight of His ministry.

When the governor of the feast was at a loss to know the source of the best wine of the feast, it is recorded that "the servants . . . knew." By their simple obedience they were brought into the center of miraculous action. It is more than likely that throughout their remaining lifetime they would glory in the fact that they had had a part in this unprecedented event, and all because of simple obedience to the Master's command.

The instruction given by the mother to the servants was "Whatsoever . . . do it." It was an order for absolute and complete obedience.

In all probability, the order to fill the pots with water seemed senseless to the servants, as did the order to "draw out . . . and bear unto the governor of the feast"; but what amazement must have been theirs when they witnessed the miraculous transformation of the water into wine, better wine than any that had been served previously at the feast.

The incident is typical of the results and value of cooperation with Christ in absolute obedience. Many are the times that one does not see the value of such obedience when the command is given, but none of His commands are meaningless. Some may appear to be foolish; but if they are His orders, they are meaningful.

It is at this point that the natural mind often rebels at the commands of God, for they seem so foolish to human thinking. Since the end cannot be seen, the process leading thereto seems unwise and is rejected.

Again this incident is typical in that the commandments of God, when obeyed, produce satisfactory results; He gives no meaningless orders, leads down no dead-end streets.

At times it seems that His ways are not best, but that is because we see only the beginning and not the end. Job had such an experience, but James tells us that at the end, Job saw "that the Lord is very pitiful, and of tender mercy" (James 5:11). It always turns out that way with those who trust and obey.

The life of absolute obedience to God is carefree and happy. One does not bear the responsibility of his own acts if they have been ordered of God.

The whole point of this incident revolves around the certainty that the Master is doing the speaking and we are dedicated to obedience; and when obedience is our purpose, we may become certain of His voice: "My sheep hear my voice" (John 10:27).

This whole way of living resolves itself into the simple pattern of knowing and doing. The struggle of self-seeking gives way to the search for His will, and the ceaseless struggle of doing is transmuted into the bearing of His easy burden.

It is noteworthy that this first of miracles wrought by Christ with the aid of menial servants produced the initial faith of His disciples that later developed into a deathless love that made them the propagators of His glorious saving gospel to the ends of the earth.

The ultimate purpose of this, His first miracle, was not revealed to His helpers. He alone knew that hence blind obedience was required of those who knew nothing of the ends He had in view.

In like manner are we unable to understand His ways and see the ends toward which He moves. Like Abraham, who "went out, not knowing whither he went" (Heb. 11:8), we are at times called upon to fill a "blind date." It is therefore imperative that we know who made the request.

The mother gave sage and permanent advice for servants of all time, advice that, if obeyed, will lead into realms of glorious victories and eternal joys.

This advice of universal obligation stands at the head of every command that Christ was to issue. It stands before us now and will to the end of time. His calls to "repent," "believe," "come," "follow," and "go" are typical of the commands to be obeyed if we are to bear the best wine to the governor of the feast.

Obedience the Highest Expression of Love

In the 13th chapter of 1 Corinthians, Paul places the crown upon the brow of love, and earlier Christ showed us what true love is and who possesses it: "He that hath my commandments, and keepeth them, he it is that loveth me: and he that loveth me shall be loved of my Father, and I will love him, and will manifest myself to him" (John 14:21). Later on, Jesus tells us that the way to stay in the love of God is to keep His commandments: "If ye keep my commandments, ye shall abide in my love; even as I have kept my Father's commandments, and abide in his love" (15:10).

If we had no other reason to know that obedience was the highest attainment open to man, it would grow from the fact that this was the avowed purpose of Jesus when He came from heaven. He said, "I came down from heaven, not to do mine own will, but the will of him that sent me" (John 6:38); and of Him it is said, "Lo, I come (in the volume of the book it is written of me,) to do thy will, O God" (Heb. 10:7). Certainly He did not propose to live His earthly life among men on any but the highest plane, nor labor at that which was secondary. True obedience to the Highest is the greatest accomplishment for man or for the Son of Man.

First: To obey is to recognize the superiority of the One you obey. Certainly the God of the universe is superior to any of His children; and when we pledge and perform that obedience, we give due recognition to that fact.

Second: In the act of obedience we take our rightful place in relation to our Maker. Any act of disobedience on our part is an assertion of superiority to the One to whom we owe allegience.

Third: Obedience aligns us with the plans and purposes of the Almighty and causes us to become partners with Him in accomplishing His purposes in life.

Fourth: We are assured of an abiding place in the kingdom of God: "He that doeth the will of God abideth for ever" (1 John 2:17).

Fifth: The only way there can be unity in the universe is for each person to be in perfect accord with the same Person. The twin truths, "No man can serve two masters" and a "house divided against itself shall not stand" drive this truth home to us (Matt. 6:24; 12:25).

The centrality of obedience in the life of Christ can be better understood when it is remembered that He came as the Second Adam. The first Adam had made shipwreck, and it was at the point of obedience that he failed. If, therefore, the failure came at the point of obedience, the restoration could come only at that point; hence, the announcement by Christ that this would be His primary concern.

Since the whole human race became involved in Adam's transgression and we are by nature disobedient, therefore the central nature of man must be changed. When he yields to God, his disobedience ends, and his life thereafter should become one of constant obedience to the divine will.

The revealed will of God in the Bible is sufficient to direct man into the ways of salvation and give him the general rules for all the activities of the Christian life; hence the Word of God must be constantly meditated upon and the aid of the Holy Spirit constantly sought so as to understand it and rightly divide it. There are, however, areas of specific and particular guidance that are not found in the Word of God. No passage in the Bible can be found to indicate what college one should attend, what girl he should marry, what occupation he should pursue, or how much money he should give in the special offering. On these matters, the Christian certainly needs guidance. Is it God's plan to give direction in such matters, or are we left to our own judgment? It is in this area of specific guidance that I am seeking to write. There are many ways that have been used by God to give direction in such matters. These have been very thoroughly explored and written upon in the past, and one scarcely needs to remention them. The writings already available in printed books may serve our purpose here. However, there seems to be but little written on the personal guidance of the Holy Spirit, so for that reason that will be the special point of emphasis here.

It seems that the one point where we fail to enter into this area of guidance is the presupposition that the speaking Voice must always be in line with what appears to be providential openings and seems to be reasonable. Special emphasis must be given to the fact that God's ways are not always apparent, nor are they in line with man's best reasoning powers. When we reduce the leadership of the Spirit to the reasonable, we eliminate the miraculous and reduce our acts to the level of human accomplishments. This we are doing in a frightful measure.

Look at the miracles of Christ. Were any of them reasonable? Was feeding 5,000 men, besides women and children, with a single lunch reasonable? Was walking on the sea a reasonable thing? Was turning gallons of water into wine an act that could be classified as reasonable? Was raising a man from the dead, who, by natural laws, had already begun to decay, a reasonable thing? Look the list over; name one miracle that He performed that you could call reasonable. What is a miracle anyway? It is something that goes beyond man's ability to perform or to understand. Miracles must go beyond reason.

As long as what is accomplished is reasonable, where does God get any credit? The works of Christ that challenged the people of His day were acts that they knew were performed by a higher power than that of man. Those who would not accept them as the works of God ascribed them to the workings of the devil, for they were compelled to ascribe them to a power that was higher than that of mere man.

What is true of the miracles of Christ is true also of the miracles performed by the disciples. Does the healing of the lame man at the Temple gate by Peter seem reasonable? Was the raising of Dorcas reasonable?

The same was true in the Old Testament: Was the calling down of fire from heaven by Elijah reasonable? Was reason leading the way when the axhead was caused to swim? Does the pulling down of the Philistines' temple by one lone man appeal to reason? What about the crossing of the Red Sea, the manna for 40 years in the wilderness, the water from the smitten rock, the Jordan crossing, the victory at Jericho? Were any of these acts of God in harmony with the best of human reason?

It is evident that when we demand that the Voice speaking to us must be reasonable in all of its commands, we rule out the supernatural. What we do may be good, but if according to our reasonings, why attribute it to God? Why use God if He is to be limited to that which can be understood by our own reasonings? This method, which it seems has been almost universally followed, that confines the leadership of the Holy Spirit to the pattern of our own thinking, has limited God in our lives and held us to a path of service explainable and understandable to man; hence, of no credit to God. Only where the acts of God can be clearly seen to go beyond the powers of man can God be truly glorified by those about us. If one is to move along the line of Spirit guidance, he must make up his mind that he cannot be guided by men. There is a place for human leadership, and there is due those in authority over us that we be in obedience to them in those areas where they have a right to command us. That is included in our total loyalty to God. I am not, however, speaking in these areas just now, but I am thinking of those personal things that relate to our own lives and on which we have a right to expect and receive guidance from the Lord alone.

We see this principle illustrated in the life of Christ. More than once did He have to turn from the advice of His best friends to follow what He knew to be the voice of His Father. We see it also in the apostle Paul who, when called of God for a task, immediately conferred not with flesh and blood but went immediately to the task that had been divinely assigned.

To be led by the Spirit, one must know that the Spirit of God has the ability to convey messages to us in a manner that can be certainly understood by us. Here is where much of the difficulty comes in. There seems to be such a dim belief that God is alive and can speak! In theory, yes; in practice, scarce. If it is true that one can know God's will for His life, and God has spoken to him and he knows that it is God, and he knows what the message is, why ask anyone? We only need help from others when we do not know ourselves what to do.

This is a dangerous doctrine, that I concede. Why? It is powerful and dynamic. There is finality in God's voice, and the world is dead set against finality in religion. They want certainty when guiding men through space, but they want no certainty in the matters of the Spirit. That is a part and outcropping of the basic problem of the human race, the desire to have one's own way. If it is admitted that God has clearly and truly spoken, then there is no place for opposition unless one openly opposes God, and there are not too many that care to be caught in doing that. As long as the matter is left to the minds of men, there is no serious problem arising from opposing it; but if from God, who can oppose? A person with orders direct from God, bent on executing them at the expense of possible loss of church, home, family, position, friends, and even of life itself, is a very dangerous person— dangerous, that is, to the kingdom of Satan and to the man-made schemes of conduct.

The person, therefore, who proposes to be led by the Spirit must be dead to the praises and criticisms of men; in short, he must be crucified to the world and have the world crucified to him, as was Paul's experience as told by him. As long as one desires that his life be lived in harmony with the crowd that he lives with, whether the crowd be worldly or Christian, he cannot be expected to know much of the leadership of the Spirit. To follow the Spirit may lead one to be quite different from his own church members. God has not made us all alike, and man's highest can only be reached by being himself plus the grace and help of God. When one begins to follow the Spirit he is following a Person, not a pattern. There is no virtue in being different just to be different. In fact, one who is different because he is following the Spirit does not note that he is different. He is normal in the eyes of the Spirit and in his own eyes.

Years ago, Jesus pointed out that faith would be hindered, in fact, destroyed, by the desire for human approval: "How can ye believe, which receive honour one of another, and seek not the honour that cometh from God only?" (John 5:44). It is this open ear to the opinions and wishes of our friends that closes our hearts to the mind and will of God. To be as others is more pleasant to the flesh, but who desires to please the flesh? Certainly not the one who has come as his Master to do the will of Him that called him.

In the light of the fact there seems to be so few professed Christians who give themselves to a fully Spirit-led life, it seems reasonable to ask the question, Why is that the case? If this question were asked to a large audience of people, there probably would be many answers and some truth in each of them; but I want to come to what I believe to be the central reason for this failure. It lies in the lack of total dedication, which involves suffering.

The Spirit of God and the spirit of the world are in two different categories, two different camps, in fact, in hostile camps. There is not as much conflict between communism and democracy as there is between the Spirit of God and the spirit of this world. More than that, it is impossible for the natural man to understand the things of the Spirit of God, and anytime one is motivated by that which those around him cannot understand, he appears to be strange and foolish; therefore, there is suffering entailed upon one who thus acts. More than that, the spirit of the world is embarrassed and confounded by the Spirit of God, and that, in turn, causes the worldling to persecute the strange-acting Christian. Unless one is dead to such treatment, he will unconsciously seek to conform his life to that of the herd and avoid embarrassment.

We have almost denied the basic cause of persecution. Some have openly said that the days of persecution of Christian people is past. They have written that off to the dark days when men were less enlightened. They say, too, that the barbarisms of the past are over—in our fair land at least—and we can expect to be at peace with all men.

In the light of these sentiments, it should be noted at what points in the life of Christ He suffered most from the Jews. It was when He began to speak of such things as His oneness with the Father, the fact that He knew the Father. In other words, when He began to emphasize the spiritual aspects of His life, they took up stones to stone Him or sought to kill Him. There is an enmity placed by God himself between the Seed of the woman and the seed of the serpent. There is no way for that to be removed as long as there are saints and sinners. The Christian's persecution arises from the fact that he is of a different order, an order hostile to the other camp. There never can be peace between the two camps. It is written that "all that will live godly in Christ Jesus shall suffer persecution" (2 Tim. 3:12).

Another problem must be faced by anyone who steps out to wholly follow the Lord and be directed by His Spirit. When one leaves the crowd and seeks to make his own way with God, he must bear the entire responsibility of his acts. As long as he can point to the fact that all of his friends are going this way, there is not much, if any, suffering involved; and if the wrong thing is done, the blame can be charged to the whole group, and but little will rest upon any one of them.

What has been said may lead the reader to believe that I am picturing the Christian's way as a hard one; that is not the case. In fact, if one really suffers persecution for Christ's sake, there is a great joy that comes from it. This way of Spirit leadership is one of relaxed peace. Jesus tells us that His yoke is easy and His burden is light; that the Christian finds to be the case. This life is to be lived in the power of Another. If the Spirit is directing, He will empower us to perform His will. The secret of the Christian life is found when one comes to rest in the will of God. The writer to the Hebrews reminds us that "there remaineth therefore a rest to the people of God" and adds, They that have entered into this rest have "ceased from [their] own works, as God did from his" (4:9-10).

Paul knew something of this "rest" when he told us that he was "striving according to his [the Spirit of God's] working" in him (Col. 1:29).

Jesus knew this law perfectly and lived by it. He denied that He did anything. He said it was His Father in Him that did the works. He had become a relaxed instrument in the hands of His Father. All He needed to know was what, where, when, and how the will of His Father was to be accomplished, and He proceeded to do it by the power of the Father in Him. It is reasonable to believe that the Lord will give His power to His children who are carrying out His purposes at His bidding and according to His plan.

Obedience, therefore, guarantees help from on high—in fact, all the help that may be needed for the execution of the Father's plan and will. Obedience itself is the guarantee of success, but obedience inevitably produces conflict. It cannot be otherwise while we live in this world and do the will of God.

The only way and the only time that the Christian and the sinners can be at peace is when the Christian ceases to press upon the sinners the claims of the gospel—in other words, when the Christian gives up the Christian warfare. The commission of each and every Christian is not altogether unlike that of Jeremiah whom God commissioned "to root out, and to pull down, and to destroy, and to throw down, to build, and to plant" (Jer. 1:10). If the Christians are aggressive in the work of the Lord, it will still be said of them, "These that have turned the world upside down are come hither also" (Acts 17:6).

This principle of *obedience that results in persecution* is almost wholly denied in our day. It should be shown that not only is its universality declared by divine inspiration when we are told that "all that will live godly in Christ Jesus shall suffer persecution," but also the very reasonableness of it is established in the very nature of the case. If we lay down the premises that the kingdom of this world is diametrically opposed to the kingdom of God, and that the Christian is commissioned to advance the kingdom of Christ at the cost of demolishing the strongholds of the enemy, and assuming the Christian is faithfully engaged in the work assigned, war cannot be avoided. Peace can be had only by compromise or by failure to contact the enemy. Conflict in a sinful world grows out of Christlikeness: "The world . . . hated me before it hated you" (John 15:18). Jesus also told His disciples, "If ye were of the world, the world would love his own: but because ye are not of the world, . . . therefore the world hateth you" (v. 19). Fundamental principles never change. This enmity started in the Garden of Eden. It was set up by God himself and will never be changed unless God changes; and He has said of himself, "I am the Lord, I change not" (Mal. 3:6).

Why then is all so quiet on the battlefront? It is because Christianity is so far removed from a total dedication to the doing of the will of God at any cost. The damning error that is blocking the way is the belief that the days of persecution are past; and anytime one would be wholly led by the Spirit but runs into some objection or suffering from the world or from the natural man, and he backs up to take the way of no suffering, he has already set to his seal that suffering is not necessary in our day.

It is utterly inconceivable that Jesus Christ would live among us today and be a hail-fellow-well-met, as most of us are. Without doubt, He would be put to death again, and that by those who profess allegiance to God. It is likewise unbelievable that the apostles would preach across this nation of ours and keep out of trouble. When they would begin to declare that there is but "one mediator between God and men" (1 Tim. 2:5), and that the mediation of salvation through a corrupt priesthood is an abomination to God, and that the statuary set up and bowed down to by millions in the name of worship to the Almighty God is plain idolatry, and those that perpetrate such doctrine are blind, leading the blind, and that the whole formula thus practiced was hatched out in hell, and that the adherents of such faith are deceived and will awaken in the bottomless pit at the end of life's day, except they repent—in short, if they should preach and demand that each individual come to Christ in his own right, and that he may have access to God through Christ, and through Him alone; and that the forgiveness of the church has no more weight or recognition in heaven than that of a bartender or a professional harlot unless it is witnessed to by the Holy Spirit within, and if thus witnessed, no other witness need be sought and paid for; *then* we would know persecution, and maybe a worse type than was witnessed in the days of the apostles. Now we condone idolatry, if not by our words, then by our silence. The masses of those who profess religion are not prepared to meet God. Jesus spoke more than once to this point. "Many will say to me in that day, Lord, Lord . . . then will I profess unto them, . . . depart from me, ye that work iniquity" (Matt. 7:22-23). He also said, "Broad is the way, that leadeth to destruction, and many there be which go in thereat"; while, said He, the way that leads to life is narrow, and "few there be that find it" (vv. 13-14). These words are disturbing, and when they are preached they disturb the sleepy souls that hear them, and sleepers do not want to be disturbed; hence, the suffering that accrues to the one that thus preaches.

Being true to God—or stating it another way, being *obedient* to God—has always caused trouble. Righteousness is a troublemaker in a world of sin. It was righteousness on the part of Abel that caused Cain to slay him. Righteousness has always produced hatred; and hatred, when matured, seeks to destroy the righteous.

Daniel Illustrates This Principle

Let us consider enough cases from the Word of God to establish the fact beyond doubt, that obedience leads to suffering; what accrues thereafter is not a point of emphasis at this time. That can be considered later. This fact that we are loathe to admit, but the one that we must not overlook, is that obedience brings suffering. It cannot be otherwise. We are engaged in warfare. To be a good soldier is to accept suffering as the inevitable; that is, if one fights. He may lie in the trenches and allow the enemy to occupy the field and avoid suffering, but he cannot arise and fight and escape it. Let us note it in Daniel.

Daniel had a set purpose to obey God and His commandments at any cost. This first showed up when he refused to eat the king's meat. When Daniel purposed in his heart that he would be obedient to the commandment of God, his purpose immediately ran counter to the plan of the king. If it had not been that God came to his rescue, he would have no doubt lost his life, for in his disobedience his life or the life of the prince of the eunuchs was at stake; and since the prince had the final word, it is evident that Daniel would have lost his life, for disobedience to a king meant death. Here the issue was drawn, and the inevitable was in sight. Only God could annul the consequences, and He did; but the fact is apparent: The purpose to obey led Daniel to the brink of destruction.

This crisis past, another awaits him. Darius had appointed Daniel to be the head over the three presidents who were over the 120 princes who were to govern the king's kingdom. Envy and jealousy began to work, and the princes and other presidents sought to dethrone Daniel. It was to his everlasting honor that his enemies admitted that the only way they could find fault with him was in his religion. In his administration and loyalty to the king, they could find no occasion to blame him. There was one point, however, where they could get him. They knew his inflexible devotion to his God and his avowed purpose to be obedient to the commandments of his God. It was this inflexible purpose to be obedient that precipitated his trouble. If only he would be less dedicated, all would be well; but his enemies were counting on his obedience, so they tricked the king into making a law that would bring Daniel's fixed purpose into face-to-face defiance of the law of the king, which according to the laws of the Medes and Persians could not be broken.

Here obedience to God was causing suffering. It was this absolute obedience, this obedience unto death, that was doing the damage. A lesser form of obedience would have averted the threatened death. Just to change this once so as to "fight and run away / And live to fight another day" instead of taking death now was, no doubt, Daniel's temptation. It is a temptation to all who would live godly and a temptation that is usually succumbed to by those who have already decided that suffering may be avoided by pursuing a more reasonable course.

Daniel was different. He loved not his life unto the death. That is why we write and think of him thousands of years after his death. He faced the issue and took the consequences of obedience that would have led inevitably to death but for divine intervention. Daniel is one who escaped death in his obedience to God. It should not be forgotten, however, that this does not establish a rule for all; for God does not see fit to deal with all alike. He has many ways to bring honor to himself and advancement to His kingdom. We do not know all the workings of His ways; therefore, we must be prepared for any eventuality. The soldier that returns from the field unscarred is not to be thought to be more heroic than the one whose lifeless form is buried on a distant battlefield. It could be that he is less heroic. Death on the field or life after the conflict is not the criterion by which loyalty and obedience can be judged.

Since we do know that God came to the rescue of Daniel, it will be well before passing him to note some of the strong points in his character—qualities that the true Christian must have.

First: He was loyal.

He was loyal to those who had a rightful authority over him. His loyalty is apparent from the fact that he was given positions of trust under three kings: Nebuchadnezzar, Belshazzar, and Darius. It plainly appears in the fact that those jealous of him and his standing with the king could find no fault with him with reference to his loyalty to the government.

Divinely led people are loyal to the government. It should be remembered that all of these kings were heathen. By them the Temple of Daniel's God at Jerusalem had been pillaged and the sacred vessels that had been dedicated to the service of Jehovah were now desecrated as vessels for wine drinking in a wild and sordid feast in the palace of a heathen enemy king. Nonetheless, Daniel was true to his government. He was practicing in Old Testament time a New Testament truth that tells us that all power is from God. He likewise knew, as he informed the king, that not only does God set up kings and dethrone them, but at times he sets up "the basest of men" (Dan. 4:17).

Second: He was fearless.

His fearlessness is revealed, when true to the revelations given to him by God, he revealed some very unpleasant truths to these wicked kings. To Nebuchadnezzar he prophesied, "They shall drive thee from men, and thy dwelling shall be with the beasts of the field, and they shall make thee to eat grass as oxen, and they shall wet thee with the dew of heaven, and seven times shall pass over thee, till thou know that the most High ruleth in the kingdom of men, and giveth it to whomsoever he will" (Dan. 4:25). This may have sobered the proud monarch for a few months, but "at the end of twelve months . . . the king spake . . . Is not this great Babylon, that I have built for the house of the kingdom by the might of my power, and for the honour of my majesty? While the word was in the king's mouth, there fell a voice from heaven, saying, O king Nebuchadnezzar, to thee it is spoken; The kingdom is departed from thee" (vv. 29-31).

To Belshazzar he said, "And thou . . . O Belshazzar, hast not humbled thine heart . . . but hast lifted up thyself against the Lord of heaven . . . and the God in whose hand thy

breath is, and whose are all thy ways, hast thou not glorified
. . . God hath numbered thy kingdom, and finished it. . . .
thou art weighed in the balances, and art found wanting"
(Dan. 5:22-23, 26-27).

In the face of the edict of Darius, he continued to pray
with his window open toward Jerusalem, knowing full well
that the decrees of a king could not be broken, and certain
death stared him in the face.

Third: Daniel was dead to the rewards of men.

When Belshazzar told Daniel, "Now if thou canst read
the writing, and make known to me the interpretation
thereof, thou shalt be clothed with scarlet, and have a chain
of gold about thy neck, and shalt be the third ruler in the
kingdom. Then Daniel answered . . . Let thy gifts be to thyself, and give thy rewards to another" (Dan. 5:16-17). In all of
his dealings, it can be said that Daniel moved in the path of
obedience to his God without fear or favor, was dead to the
honor of any person, and cared not for the emoluments of
time.

Fourth: Daniel was faithful in his testimony for God.

When the dreams of Nebuchadnezzar could not be remembered and all the wise men of the realm admitted that
they could not bring it to his memory, Daniel doubtless heard
their verdict, "There is not a man upon the earth that can
shew the king's matter . . . and there is none other that can
shew it before the king, except the gods, whose dwelling is
not with flesh" (Dan. 2:10-11). Daniel declared, "But there is
a God in heaven that revealeth secrets" (v. 28).

Before Belshazzar, he recounted the glory of his father's
kingdom and reminded him that "the most high God gave
Nebuchadnezzar thy father a kingdom and majesty, and
glory, and honour" (Dan. 5:18), and it was God who took it
away. Speaking to Darius from the den of lions, he said, "My
God hath sent his angel, and hath shut the lions' mouths,

that they have not hurt me" (6:22). On all occasions he gave due recognition to God, even though he was in a heathen country, where Jehovah was not worshiped.

Fifth: Daniel was a man of humility.

When He had triumphed over all the wise men of the kingdom and might have taken credit to himself, he was forward to tell the king, "But as for me, this secret is not revealed to me for any wisdom that I have more than any living" (Dan. 2:30). In the ninth chapter of Daniel, there is a very earnest prayer of confession for Israel. Some of the statements are, "We have sinned . . . committed iniquity . . . done wickedly . . . neither have we hearkened unto thy servants the prophets . . . to us belongeth confusion of face, to our kings, to our princes, and to our fathers . . . Neither have we obeyed the voice of the Lord our God." On and on he goes confessing, but the remarkable thing about his prayer of confession is that he included himself in it. He said, "And whiles I was speaking, and praying, and confessing *my* sin and the sin of my people Israel" (vv. 5-6, 8, 10, 20, italics added). His honesty and humility cannot escape us.

Sixth: Daniel was a man of faith.

After the day of execution was postponed for the wise men that Daniel might have time to get a revelation of the king's secret from the Lord, when he and his companions had prayed and received the answer, he went to Arioch and told him, "I will shew unto the king the interpretation" (Dan. 2:24).

This reveals the results of a faith that they had that brought an answer, but what is more remarkable is that Daniel told the king before they prayed "that he would shew the king the interpretation" (Dan. 2:16). Then again, when Daniel was called in before Belshazzar to interpret the handwriting on the wall, he said to the king, "I will read the writing unto the king, and make known to him the interpretation" (5:17).

When Daniel was taken up out of the lions' den, it was said, "No manner of hurt was found upon him, because he believed in his God" (Dan. 6:23). The only reason that I remember that Jesus ascribed for the destruction of faith was, "How can ye believe, which receive honour one of another, and seek not the honour that cometh from God only?" (John 5:44). It is evident from facts already cited herein that Daniel was free from the desire for man's honor to a marked degree.

Thus we see that Daniel, the loyal, fearless, but humble servant of God, dead to the honors of men and always ready to give praise unto his God, met possible demotion and death to be obedient to the will of his Master.

Elijah, Another Example of Trouble Because of Obedience

Elijah spoke to Ahab in the name of the Lord, "As the Lord God of Israel liveth, before whom I stand, there shall not be dew nor rain these years, but according to my word" (1 Kings 17:1). The Lord knew that this was the signal for trouble for His messenger, so He told him to hide. The danger was imminent. Ahab searched for him in all the countries round about. Jezebel threatened, "So let the gods do to me, and more also, if I make not thy life as the life of one of [the dead prophets of Baal] by to morrow about this time" (19:2). Elijah knew that his prophecy in the name of the Lord would be dangerous. He had seen the results of the prophecies of other prophets who had spoken in the name of the Lord. He reminded in his prayer, "The children of Israel have forsaken thy covenant, thrown down thine altars, and slain thy prophets with the sword; and I, even I only, am left; and they seek my life, to take it away" (v. 10). While Elijah showed some signs of cowardice, nevertheless he did obey the Lord and deliver the message; and it was this obedience that produced the trouble, which is the point at issue.

Take the Case of Micaiah—1 Kings 22:7-28

God had determined the death of the wicked king, Ahab. He was going into battle against the king of Syria. Jehoshaphat, the king of Judah, had joined him in this venture. Before going into battle, "Jehoshaphat said unto the king of Israel, Enquire, I pray thee, at the word of the Lord to day" (v. 5). Ahab called the prophets together—about 400 men—and with one accord they prophesied that Ahab would be victorious in the oncoming battle. Jehoshaphat, being more religious, felt that something was not quite right, so he asked Ahab if there was not another prophet. There was one more. He had not been called. The record is that Ahab hated him.

Micaiah was called. Those sent to get him informed him that 400 prophets had spoken victory in the name of the Lord, and of course, he would want to be with the crowd. His answer is illuminating: "As the Lord liveth, what the Lord saith unto me, that will I speak" (v. 14). He knew that the king hated him. He knew also the probable fate of anyone who opposed the king, and he had been urged by those who had been sent for him, "Let thy word, I pray thee, be like the word of one of them, and speak that which is good" (v. 13). The cost of being obedient was apparent, but he obeyed.

The verdict came, "Thus saith the king, Put this fellow in the prison, and feed him with bread of affliction and with water of affliction, until I come in peace" (v. 27). The suffering came from his obedience.

Jeremiah Is a Case at Hand

The Lord called Jeremiah to be a prophet and told him plainly, "They shall fight against thee" (Jer. 1:19). This came to pass. "The princes were wroth with Jeremiah, and smote him, and put him in prison in the house of Jonathan the scribe" (37:15). This was not the end of his prison days. He prophesied the capture of the city by the army of Babylon; "Then took they Jeremiah, and cast him into the dungeon of

Malchiah" (38:6). Obedience to the command of the Lord was the source of his trouble.

It would not be wise to go further in enumerating cases. These should be conclusive proof that the prophets of the Old Testament encountered persecution, imprisonment, and at times, death because of their obedience to God.

Let Nehemiah sum up the situation for the Old Testament prophets; he complains, "They [Israel] were disobedient, and rebelled against thee, and cast thy law behind their backs, and slew thy prophets which testified against them to turn them to thee" (Neh. 9:26).

Stephen, commenting on the same situation, said, "Which of the prophets have not your fathers persecuted? and they have slain them which shewed before of the coming of the Just One" (Acts 7:52).

Jesus advised His followers to rejoice when they were persecuted, adding, "For so persecuted they the prophets which were before you" (Matt. 5:12). Jesus also charged the Jews of His day, "Ye are the children of them which killed the prophets" (23:31). This matter of suffering for obedience was no isolated case in the days of the Old Testament saints.

Did all this change when the light of the gospel of Christ broke upon the world? Nay, it increased. Obedience to God brought prison sentences to Peter, James, John, Paul, and others. It brought death to 10 of the apostles, and death to millions who followed in their footsteps of obedience. Christian suffering ceases only when we cease to war against sin.